A dare: read just the introduction to this book. A bet: you won't be able to put it down. Karissa's funny, poignant, tender, searing memoir/theology of singleness deserves a place alongside Ann Lamott's *Traveling Mercies* and Lauren Winner's *Girl Meets God*—for the beauty of its writing, for the depths of its insights, and most of all for its power to change our minds. I dearly wish I'd had this book when I was a pastor, and Karissa was part of my church! I'm deeply grateful I have it now and can repent of all the nonsense I've thought, and sometimes spoken, about singleness. This is a book for singles, yes, and in Karissa you have a kind, wise, often wisecracking guide. But it's also, maybe more so, a book for pastors, professors, and ministry leaders—really, for anybody who has ears to hear and needs fresh eyes to see.

—Mark Buchanan
author of *The David Trilogy*

In this book, Karissa Sovdi offers a gift to the Church and all the single people found within. And that is this reminder: "Singleness is not a problem to be solved. It is a life to be lived." Cutting through the cacophony of messages about marriage and family, which can make unmarried people feel less-than or as if they are consigned to a lifelong waiting room, Sovdi helps readers live a life of purpose, fun, adventure, and faithfulness right now, no matter their marital status. It's not about waiting. It's about living.

—Karen Stiller
author of *Holiness Here: Searching for God in the Ordinary Events of Everyday Life*
www.karenstiller.com

KARISSA SOVDI

SURVIVING *Christianity* UNMARRIED

A THEOLOGY OF SINGLENESS
THAT ISN'T LOOKING FOR ITS CURE

SURVIVING CHRISTIANITY UNMARRIED
Copyright © 2025 by Karissa Sovdi

All rights reserved. Neither this publication nor any part of this publication may be reproduced or transmitted in any form or by any means, electronic or mechanical, including photocopying, recording or any information storage and retrieval system, without permission in writing from the author.

Unless otherwise indicated, scriptures taken from the Holy Bible, New International Version®, NIV®. Copyright © 1973, 1978, 1984, 2011 by Biblica, Inc.™ Used by permission of Zondervan. All rights reserved worldwide. www.zondervan.com The "NIV" and "New International Version" are trademarks registered in the United States Patent and Trademark Office by Biblica, Inc.™ Scripture quotations are from the ESV® Bible (The Holy Bible, English Standard Version®), © 2001 by Crossway, a publishing ministry of Good News Publishers. Used by permission. All rights reserved. The ESV text may not be quoted in any publication made available to the public by a Creative Commons license. The ESV may not be translated in whole or in part into any other language. Verses marked NASB are taken from the New American Standard Bible®, Copyright © 1960, 1971, 1977, 1995, 2020 by The Lockman Foundation. All rights reserved.

Soft cover ISBN: 978-1-4866-2651-9
Hard cover ISBN: 978-1-4866-2652-6
eBook ISBN: 978-1-4866-2653-3

Word Alive Press
119 De Baets Street Winnipeg, MB R2J 3R9
www.wordalivepress.ca

Cataloguing in Publication information can be obtained from Library and Archives Canada.

*To anyone who has doubted their worth
because of their relationship status.*

INTRODUCTION ix

PART ONE: GRIEVE THE FAIRY TALE 1
ONE: The Glass Slipper Finally Breaks 3
TWO: The Half-Life 9
THREE: A Purpose, Not a Reason 15

PART TWO: RECKON WITH DESIRE 33
FOUR: The Elephant in the Room 35
FIVE: Why This Christian Single Is Done with Saving Sex 37
SIX: Managing a Non-Sex Life 43
SEVEN: The Desires of Your Heart 65
EIGHT: Open to Love 75
NINE: My Choice 83
TEN: God's Choice 89

PART THREE: LEARN HOW TO BE A PERSON 95
ELEVEN: The Bible Is for Me: Confessions of an Accidental Feminist 97
TWELVE: Following the Leader: How Jesus Did Singleness 105
THIRTEEN: Experiencing Loneliness 121
FOURTEEN: Practicing the Art of Friendship 129

PART FOUR: EMBRACE A NEW REALITY 151
FIFTEEN: Loving What Is 153
SIXTEEN: Champagne Moments 163
SEVENTEEN: Seen 169
A Letter to Twenty-Year-Old Me 175
Truly Loved 177

ACKNOWLEDGEMENTS 179
ENDNOTES 181

INTRODUCTION

IF YOU'RE ANYTHING like me, before even considering a book like this, you already flipped to the About the Author section or ran a quick Google search to find out whether I'm single. I'm not sure what you found, but I can assure you this was not written from the comfort of a white-picketed home with a husband, 1.8 kids, and a dog. At the time of writing this, I'm single. As single as they come! I'm the walking statistic of the twentysomething turned thirtysomething Christian woman who can't land a man because men aren't in church and need to man up, or because women are eating their feelings and need to slim down, or because my youth group did one too many Bible studies on courtship and I have unrealistic expectations of dating, or because of whatever other reason that's trending in Christian media right now.

What you're about to read has been over a decade in the making. I just didn't know it at the time I started. These are the words I searched for on shelves and online inventories of Christian bookstores through most of my twenties—until I gave up, realizing they didn't yet exist. I've since learned that I needed to make them exist.

This book has been generated from many creative forms, including song lyrics, stand-up comedy routines, essays, blogs, letters, reels, speeches, sermons, and even the draft outline of a one-woman show. But mostly it has been gathered from the rich conversations and informal interviews I've had with the amazing single people I've had the privilege to know. Among the results are many joyful and painful revelations of how to be both a Christ follower and a single adult at the same time in a Christian culture that tends to speak to adults only in the context of the nuclear family.

Single people now outnumber married people in North America, and many of them live on their own. Yet it is rare for a church to reflect these statistics demographically, programmatically, or theologically. This is a problem that simply cannot continue if we are to advance the mission of love to which we are called. For the message of Jesus to serve as good news to the world we serve, Christians everywhere need to care about whether our communities include space in which singles can belong. And for us singles to thrive and find community, we need to be surrounded by attitudes and messages that don't consider us second best. For the church to be truly inclusive, our focus in training up children, youth, and young adults has to be about more than preparing them for romance and reproduction.

This book is not about dating, marriage, or finding a way out of singleness, though all those topics will be addressed; it is about exploring a theology of singleness that isn't looking for its cure. I do not advocate for singles ministry or champion the disparagement of marriage or family, but I do attempt to elevate a status that is largely and unbiblically overlooked.

The following is a labour of love to the many singles I have encountered who question their worth and purpose because of their relationship status. I think of it as being written to the church, whether or not the readership is ever that wide, as I think the principles can help inform the broader church family about what it's like to be single and how to do a better job of supporting singles.

I don't claim to represent all Christian singles—I'm not divorced, widowed, a single parent, or older than forty and I realize others will differ in terms of theology, relationship history, cultural heritage, income, and living situation—but I do share as much as I can of the experience of singleness and general themes I've discovered in my own life and from those around me. Whoever you are, you are welcome to read, enjoy, ponder, and argue with everything here, taking what works and leaving what doesn't. Perhaps you've figured this all out on your own, much faster and more easily. At the very least, my hope is that you won't have to browse the book inventories for as long as I did.

If you're proximal to my position on the topic of singleness, I hope this is affirming. If you're where I was ten years ago, I hope it's inspiring, if not instructional, and can save you some heartache and angst. If you're where

I will be ten years from now, I hope this is adorable, and that we can meet some day for you to share with me what I don't yet know. If you're anyone or anywhere else, may this inform and spur you to consider the singles in your lives in a new light and wonder how you might encourage others to do the same.

PART ONE

GRIEVE THE *Fairy Tale*

THE GLASS SLIPPER FINALLY BREAKS

*If you are brave enough to say goodbye, life will
reward you with a new hello.*[1]
—Paulo Coelho

THE FIRST WEEK is strictly about coping, a breathe-in, breathe-out, one-foot-in-front-of-the-other kind of functioning. Somewhere around hour thirty-six of the kind of crying that has me Googling how many tears the human eye can produce before causing dehydration, I realize that it could very well be the longest consecutive amount of time I've ever cried, a realization over which I cry some more, because surely I should have cried the most when my grandmother died.

These musings, along with a few gluttonous hours of television, seem to reduce the sting, but I know it will take only an instant of inattention from these distractions for everything to flood back, both the tears and instant replays.

After the crying finally stops, the trance breaks, at least enough for me to discover the dirty dishes, unmade bed, scattered laundry, and discarded footwear, all evidence that I have at some point eaten and slept and maybe even gone outside. So I busy myself with the aftermath of my first round of distractions. I dust cookie crumbs from the coffee table, gather strewn tissues for the garbage, and recycle the junk mail I don't remember collecting. I run a dishwasher full of mugs and spoons, and a washer full of pyjamas and yoga pants. I rinse the bubble-bath residue from the tub that has been my sanctuary for three days and pause long enough before the bathroom mirror to assemble my neglected hair into a ponytail.

And as the dryer finishes humming, the dishwasher finishes whirring, and the teakettle gives a final sigh of relief, I finally hear what I've been afraid of for days: silence. It's the kind that makes my ears hurt from straining to hear something other than my own heartbeat, a sound I find annoyingly assuring. It's as if my own body, specifically my broken heart, is trying to convey to me the truth I haven't wanted to face—that life does go on. Because, regardless of the state of my kitchen, hair, or favourite TV characters, still here under the blue duvet next to the saucer with the soggy peppermint teabag, I sit.

Single.

Singlehood may come more easily to some than to others. For example, those who didn't play fake wedding at five years old may have an easier time of it. If you grew up with a marriage-first, family-centred worldview like I did, it was probably tougher. Evangelicalism especially has a way of training men and women to be husbands and wives almost from infancy. But I would hazard to guess that regardless of one's single story, there are always components of it that feel accidental. Whether single intentionally, whether previously coupled, there are just some aspects of singleness that don't seem to be part of the script.

Perhaps for you, it was realizing there were chores around the house, yard, garage, or home office that you didn't know you would have to do. Maybe you discovered desires that surprised you, and you fear you might not be able to satisfy them alone. Possibly you've reached age milestones for which you had other intentions, or encountered decisions you assumed would be made cooperatively.

However these accidentals may register, it gradually dawns on you that you may do much, or possibly all, of your adult life uncoupled.

Some try to accept this with a certain air of grace and dignity. Maybe you slowly stop naming the age you plan to be married by, or casually stop participating in fantasy wedding planning or the name-that-future-baby game. You find a way to calm your panic attacks over having to sign legal or financial documents alone. You begrudgingly pay for a handyman or housecleaner... or learn to be handy and clean, or live with crooked pictures and dirty bathrooms. Maybe you become more career-focused and ever so subtly make future-based statements more tentative. For instance, "When I have kids" may transform into "If I ever have children."

But in the gradual dawning of this realization, there are also likely some booms and crashes—or in my case, a quarter-life crisis.

For me, Plan A was always marriage. From the dress-up trunk and Barbie castle of my hallowed childhood playroom, I invented husbands, weddings, pregnancies, and families, a life of wifery and motherhood that was well exemplified in my home by a most excellent mother of five. Smitten at fifteen, dating at sixteen, engaged at nineteen, married at twenty, and pregnant at twenty-two, my mom had the only life I ever considered wanting. In fairness to her, this was the life promoted to me in pretty much every other circle I found myself in, whether church or as the audience of the pre-2000 Disney princesses who found true love before they could drive a magic carpet.

So when my sixteenth birthday arrived without any prospects, I subconsciously assumed that Mr. Right had spotted me at some point from the sidelines of my life and would land on my doorstep during my birthday party, having already sought my dad's permission to court me of course, and we would live happily ever after.

By high school graduation, there was still no knight in shining armour. I had made some career plans, but only so I would have a financial safety net in case my husband's career couldn't support our young family entirely. As if ignorant of the fact that I was still missing the key component of my plan, I dismissed any options that might be more conducive to finding a husband, such as Bible college, and assumed that my prince would magically appear once my second-income training was complete.

Sometime during my second semester of university, it dawned on me that my great plan to know my future husband for five years before marrying at twenty definitely wasn't going to happen. My career pursuit began to mean more to me than diligently carrying out Operation: Housewife, and by the time I finished my first degree I had even learned a party line to satisfy the pitiful glares I received from those who noticed the unadorned third finger of my left hand: I was glad there was no pesky male around to distract me from whatever pursuit I was occupied with at the time.

The first four years after university graduation were a mix of milestones and unacknowledged disillusionment. I worked professionally, purchased a home, ran a ministry, and dabbled in the entertainment industry, but I still framed all this success, failure, and independence as an alternate life as I covertly pursued my real plan. Having never fully embraced my single status, I found myself living half of two different lives.

It took me far too long to realize that neither was very fun. I was both the world's least career-driven university graduate on account of my desire for domestication, as well as the least successful pastor's daughter on the planet for not attaining it.

If avoiding singleness is one's ultimate priority, then every other accomplishment or experience is somehow suboptimal and may seem like settling for less. In other words, if marriage is always Plan A, every other aspect of life is automatically demoted to Plan B. That is a problem when your whole life is defined as "not marriage."

Thus the meltdown.

I guess the tears came in response to a breakup of sorts, but my tissues and crumb-laden carpets were about more than a particular two-years-too-late, define-the-relationship conversation, beginning with "We need to talk" and ending with me in the seemingly permanent role of best friend. It was about more than one person, situationship, or relational disappointment; I was mourning an entire state of being. I had spent my early adulthood living in a life that didn't fit, a life built around an idea of what life should be.

So it was at the end of my fourth—and hopefully final—failure to become the girl next door whose best friend accidentally fell in love with her, and at the beginning of my ninth year of being *legally* single (old enough to date, yet not dating), I finally *had enough*. Enough of being relegated to the friend zone, of playing the role of surrogate girlfriend in a kind of husband-grooming dress rehearsal for my male friends to polish their skills before finding someone else. Enough of the insane fantasy that had me turning every ringless man in a thirty-kilometre radius into a potential spouse. Enough of unconsciously viewing every other woman as a source of envy or competition. Enough of the placeholder job I only endured because it would fit around a future family. Enough of the house that was too big and expensive for me to do anything with but stay home and notice empty rooms, the city with all the men I had failed to secure, and the debt I'd incurred from earning the degree I wasn't using. Enough of feeling trapped with a husband-sized hole still waiting to be filled. Enough of watching my life pass by as I waited for it to start.

I was at the climax of my anti-fairytale. And while anyone can have their romance bubble burst, the single person must slowly realize there is no white horse, no knight, and no damsel. There is only the fact that glass slippers really hurt your feet and are perhaps worth leaving behind.

THE HALF-LIFE

When you discover you've been leading only half a life, the other half is going to haunt you until you develop it.[2]
—Phillips Brooks

I CAME BY my path-to-the-altar worldview honestly. My childhood was primed with stories of my parents' high school and Bible college romance, as well as the regular montage of 80s and 90s schoolgirl fairytales. My adolescence was punctuated by a promise ring and the purity movement. My early college years were peppered with wedding invitations.

For the sake of full disclosure, my thirties seemed to be peppered with just as many divorce announcements.

Each time I approached an age that I thought should have been accompanied by a relational milestone, I felt the assault on my assumptive world. I woke up at sixteen without a boyfriend, at nineteen without a fiancé, at twenty without a husband, and at twenty-three without children. However honestly I came by my initial rose-coloured perspective, somewhere between my first broken heart and umpteenth solo New Year's Eve, I decided that my marriage paradigm wasn't working for me anymore. For better or worse, I was over feeling like a perpetual half-couple.

For me, this epiphany resulted in some drastic decisions. I relocated, sight unseen, to a new city in a new province. I sold most of what I owned and paid off my student debt. I quit my job—quit my life, as it was—and started over.

This may sound adventurous and even glamorous, and some of it actually was, but for the most part it just meant going back to square one—sharing living space, taking the bus, working menial jobs, finding a new church, and building a circle of friends. This was essentially round two of all the things I had done post-university except for one key difference: this time I wasn't waiting for Mr. Right to swoop in and complete the picture.

Contrary to what some of my friends thought, I wasn't rebounding from a breakup. I was rebelling against the entire concept of an incomplete life. Much like athletes are coached to envision themselves achieving what they want—their ball going in the net, their body vaulting over the pole, their strokes propelling them down the swimming lane—I had invested so much of my time and energy visualizing life as a married woman. And just as the Olympic athlete who doesn't place must mourn the medals they didn't win, I had to grieve the loss of my anticipated life.

It may be easy to dismiss singleness as a fact of life when you're younger. But as the expectation of a singleness expiration date takes hold, it's difficult not to shape your decisions around it. After years of building a life that would be conducive to a family state, I determined to make a life I could enjoy all on my own. This meant seriously shifting gears and perspectives. Some called me brave. Others, I'm sure, thought I was being irresponsible. But I needed to test the limits of my independence to see how far it would take me.

Such extremes may not be required for everyone. The more I explore singleness, though, the more I'm convinced that a single person must grieve their unintentional life before they can pursue an intentional one. We must host ourselves through the death of a dream. The goal is not to stop imagining our futures but, in fact, to reimagine them. This may involve grieving the loss of specific relationships, people, and opportunities, but it goes further and takes into account the lives we visualized.

I had to grieve being single before I could enjoy being single. I had to mourn my imaginary romance and wedding and husband and home before I could move on without them. I had to let myself be angry and sad and confused by the independence I hadn't asked for before I could stop resenting it and start embracing it.

While I have done a lot of this work—allowing myself to wrestle with uncomfortable truths, realizing that some dreams might never come true, denying, bargaining, raging, and crying—I can still be surprised at how grief is not static. It can sneak up on me in the middle of a fantastic weekend with my girlfriends and make me feel lonely. Some birthdays are celebrations and others are empty reminders of what I don't have. I can find contentment in the prospect of never getting married, then remember that this could mean I never get to be a mother. Some days I'm giddy with independence and other days I find myself choking back tears over ticking the single status box on a tax form or purchasing a queen-sized mattress just for me. I still sometimes break down in the grocery store at the random recognition that I may always cook for one. I see that there may be a ritual involved in combining romantic comedies with junk food on Friday nights. Through all this, I've learned to be gentler with myself when I'm upset.

As I've learned to characterize my disappointment as grief, I've been able to recognize those times when I oscillate between two realities— accepting and embracing my single life and its adventures and feeling sadness at the lack of companionship and family I thought I would now have. When I'm greeted by an empty apartment after a significant day, with no one to debrief, I feel the sting of loneliness and let tears run down my face. When I attend a Christian function and am made to feel like a novelty or minority, the lens of grief empowers me to balance advocacy with compassion for myself and those to whom I am constantly explaining my experience. When I feel a lump in my throat during a romantic scene in a silly movie, the voice of grief whispers, "It's okay to be sad." When I'm sick or see an elderly person struggling, I may have a flash of fear of dying alone. Sometimes grief comes early, in bite-sized pieces, to make it easier to digest.

My life circles back to the topic of coupledom often. Most times, I don't even notice and handle it with grace. Other times, I greet it with a tantrum. Such is the nature of grief.

Embracing and grieving the single life aren't mutually exclusive behaviours. Whether single or not, there will always be tension between imagining our futures and embracing reality. If you've been visualizing a future that relies heavily on things you can't influence or control, and if you've shaped your present around it, then you either have to maintain the façade or grieve your own unmet expectations. I'm talking about facing the life you thought you would have, as well as the current state you didn't exactly plan. These are losses, gaps between our hopes and the actualities we are left to deal with. If they aren't grieved, they will haunt us—or more specifically, they will hold us back from the life that's possible.

To say this another way, if you have so far built your single life around a spouse-shaped hole, you have to reckon with the ensuing emptiness.

As with many losses, this grief may extend to those around you. Those who love you or have expectations of your future may struggle with how your have-nots impact them. Perhaps one or both of your parents thought they would have in-laws and grandchildren by now. Or maybe you've stumbled into a new parent-child dynamic because your experiences have surpassed those who have no idea what it's like to be single at your age. Maybe your siblings or friends thought you would have coupledom in common when meeting up for dinner. It's possible your church doesn't know what to do with you.

You can have grace for these losses, but you may not be able to fix them. For me, as I've accepted my reality, it's become simpler to ask those around me to enroll in the new normal, and not to worry if they don't.

The tricky part, of course, is that this new normal doesn't mean the matter is ever really resolved, since the possibility of coupledom is always on the table. The grief of singleness confounds closure, as one must come to grips with the fact that marriage may never happen while facing the possibility that it always could. While we may wish to see the future and know definitively whether our singleness is permanent, the way through is simply to live the life that's set before us in the best way we can. Sometimes this means going to God and thanking him for what is. Sometimes it means going to God and asking him for something different. Often it means going to God and just allowing our pain to exist in his presence as we sit before him and say our version of "Ouch!"

I've seen many marriages falter when partners can't let go of their single mindsets. I've come to understand that hanging onto the idea of marriage can ruin singleness in the same way that hanging onto singleness can ruin a marriage. I'm not suggesting that successful singleness requires a person to give up all hope of coupledom, become embittered, and swear off romance. But I do suggest that we must stop putting our lives on hold. We can be filled with expectancy while letting go of our expectations. We can be enthralled with possibility while letting go of the ideas that limit us.

It's just that finding a new perspective and coming to a place of acceptance may first require us to make some space to deny, barter, rage, and ugly-cry.

A PURPOSE, NOT A REASON

The formulation of the problem is often more essential than its solution...[3]
—Albert Einstein

WHEN PEOPLE ASK me about being single, I usually feel as if they're asking me about a rash I've had trouble curing, one for which they have the perfect remedy: "Oh, you're still single? Have you tried putting Polysporin on it?" Except what they say is, "Have you tried online dating?" "Do you think it's because men find you too intimidating?" "You should put yourself out there more." After I've accomplished something significant, some may ask, "how are you still single?" This is even more common when the accomplishment is domestic, such as cooking an amazing dinner. All I can do is bite my tongue and hold back the sarcastic retort: "I don't know, but I bet it would be fun to analyze my flaws for an hour!"

Some adages are more grim. "You're not getting any younger," or "Aren't you afraid of dying alone?" Others try to offer a modicum of hope, but the hope is always rooted in finding a match: "There's someone for everyone," "God will send you someone when you're ready," "Enjoy this season," "Singleness is a gift," "Just keep praying for your future spouse," "Become who you want to attract," "It happens when you least expect it," and so on.

So to summarize, like a kid in a candy store not thinking about dessert, I just need to stop expecting romance while also praying for it every day and trust the Lord with my gift while also putting myself out there out of a fear of dying alone... but wait, don't more than half of people die alone? Or are there couples out there planning their deaths precisely so they can shuffle off this mortal coil at the exact same moment?

Well-intentioned advice for singles is available in droves, and most of it is premarital. In fact, most resources, seminars, and events I've heard about that are targeted explicitly to singles have turned out to be more about how to get unsingle. I've taught myself to see all this content as amusing, and maybe even being motivated out of love, but I'm increasingly perplexed as to how and why we continually measure singles against the yardstick of marriage.

Singleness is not a problem, period. This reality demands to be reiterated often to a world that finds insecurity in aloneness, as well as to a Christian culture focused so intently on an ancient approach to family that they forget about their founders' approach to faith. We often glorify coupledom, marriage, and family to the extent of devaluing the state of singleness. We even pathologize it.

But singleness is not a problem to be solved. It is a life to be lived.

At the same time, we mistakenly cast marriage as a static solution rather than an ongoing process. I have come to see this as a deficit-mindset. It discourages the single person from embracing their present life by pushing them to search for the cause of their singleness and identify a cure. It also sets people up for marriage failure by cultivating a misunderstanding of both the human condition and our ultimate source of peace and fulfilment.

What if the church could foster a theology of singleness that doesn't look for a cure?

This reminds me of a moment in the political drama *The West Wing*. Martin Sheen's character, President Bartlet, talks about why many Americans vote for tax cuts that will only impact the top one percent of earners: "It doesn't matter if most voters don't benefit. They all believe that someday they will. That's the problem with the American dream. It makes everyone concerned for the day they're gonna be rich."[4]

I would argue that the dream of marriage has a similar effect on singles. In imagining that we'll be married someday, we can forfeit the value of what exists now for the allure of what might come next. We may even choose against our own interests and diminish the enjoyment of our single existences for the sake of protecting an unguaranteed future.

It's time to raise the profile of singleness. In doing so, our aim is not to disparage marriage but to be able to see both coupled and uncoupled states as important, sacred, and valuable. Neither presents a direct path or barrier to living a fulfilled, Christ-centred, God-blessed life. Neither is to be held up as the only way. Neither is easy. Both require commitment, sacrifice, and the help of the Holy Spirit. What we miss when pursuing either extreme is the reality that marriage isn't for everyone, singleness is not for everyone, and coveting someone else's life always gets us into trouble.

As disconcerting as this may be, perhaps the most freeing revelation I've had as a single adult is that marriage is not inevitable. As I've slowly and sometimes painfully digested this fact, several related falsities have unravelled for me, and I think they may be helpful to others.

LIE #1: THERE MUST BE A REASON YOU'RE SINGLE

No doubt the portions of my story you've read so far have provoked you to deduce some rationale for my single status. I'm sure I come to similar conclusions every time I try to write an online dating profile without sounding like a Bible-thumping cat lady or too-busy-for-love career woman who shouldn't have time to be on the apps. But if I could action a wish or prayer for other singles, it would be that they not waste needless hours, days, and even years looking for the reason they're still single—and if I could commission a command to all the friends, family, and colleagues of those singles, it would be to stop asking for one.

In a person's late teens and early adult years, it may not be required to provide an explanation for one's singleness. This phase of life is expected to be focused on pursuing dreams, education, and careers. But there is a subtle turning point when the term single becomes a label, and an ill-fitting one at that. Suddenly, admitting to being single is uncomfortable and requires justification. A single woman once told me that she faces this onslaught so often that it feels like harassment.

The single life has often been a challenge for people of faith. Paul, a pioneer of the early church, elevated singleness as a preferred state (1 Corinthians 7:38). It's interesting to consider how this would have flown in the face of Paul's Jewish culture, which so valued the nuclear family.

In emulation of this saint, not to mention Christ himself, Catholics often promote singleness and celibacy as the ultimate form of consecration. Perhaps they do so for less-than-reverent political and economic reasons. In any event, this view has taken much criticism for being extreme and has been blamed for many improprieties. However, it stands as an example that marriage was not always the default Christian destination.

At some point in its disdain for this approach, evangelicals have dragged the pendulum to the opposite extreme, elevating marriage as the one-flesh union to be beat (Genesis 2:24). If singleness is ever embraced in this context, it's usually only on temporary terms and most likely as some kind of premarital lesson. If you don't believe me, I wonder how many churches you can think of where the lead pastor has never been married. With the exception of widows and widowers, an espoused status has worked its way into the unwritten job description for those in Christian leadership.

It's ironic when you consider that our ultimate leader, Christ himself, never took a wife.

When marriage and family are elevated in this way, it's easy to dismiss singleness as the result of a lesser faith. In accordance with a name-it-claim-it theology, many singles carry shame about their relationship status, attributing it to a lack of faith. Statements embracing singleness can be perceived to superstitiously work against the desired state of marriage.

But what if you aren't single because of a lack of faith? What if you aren't single because of anything? What if you're just single?

The truth is that there are many reasons to be single. Some involve social constructs and trends, such as coupling age, patriarchy, feminism, and the economy. Some reasons relate to a person's choice to prioritize personal or professional aspirations over romantic ones. Some have to do with shifts in social norms, the isolating effect of technology, the commodification of dating through apps and algorithms, and cultural shifts in understanding and treatment of gender and sexuality. Some reasons carry sorrow resulting from death and divorce. Some are accompanied by complicating factors such as physical challenges or single parenthood. We can speculate endlessly on people's personal failings, commitment avoidance, and general baggage.

Yet despite these many reasons, people couple up every day. And many of the supposed problems associated with singleness, such as loneliness or selfishness, are individual issues that go beyond relationship status. When marriage isn't inevitable, singleness doesn't require an explanation.

LIE #2: SINGLENESS HAS TO BE USEFUL

Identifying specific reasons for singleness isn't the issue, since there are many. The problem is the need to find a reason. Singleness may have to be grieved, but being single isn't inherently terrible just because you don't like it. By constantly trying to determine why we're single, we fall into the trap of utilitarianism, only valuing aspects of our lives for their usefulness.

Not everything in life needs to have a use. Trying to find the utility of a thing often results in prioritizing logic over art, function over beauty, and evidence over elegance. Utilitarianism fails to recognize the majesty of God. It also opens the door to feeling shame around using our singleness productively. The single person who can't draw a direct line between their singleness and their value to the kingdom may feel as though they've failed.

God can have purposes for your life without explaining them to you. A Christian needs only to spend a little time studying the sciences to draw the conclusion that many aspects of the universe reveal a God who often seems to like pretty, interesting things just because. As a good, gift-giving Father, he often springs for the lavish fashion accessory or funky piece of art over sensible sneakers and reusable Tupperware.

When we overvalue the usefulness of a thing, we can fall prey to the same kind of flawed thinking the Pharisees used when watching the woman wash Jesus's feet with her tears, dry them with her hair, and anoint them with perfume (Luke 7:36–50). A utilitarian view perceives the use of expensive perfume to be wasteful, whereas Jesus saw it as an extravagant expression of love.

A person's relationship status need not be inherently useful. Rather, as individuals, we find our purpose in living stories that edify others and glorify God in all states. Relationship status is a single plot point in the narrative, not the sole focus of one's character development.

Trying to find a reason or use for singleness can also exert pressure on every other aspect of a person's life. Especially with the rise of influencer culture, it's easy to think that we must outperform those around us to prove that we have value. According to social media, after all, I can't just be unattached; I have to either spend every moment of my unattachment trying to find a romantic partner or actively demonstrate how disruptive a relationship would be to the various aspects of my life. On top of that, as a Christian single, I also have to show how useful my spiritual life and ministry are.

The search for utility isn't easily or enduringly satisfied, and a person's relationship status is no exception. In Christian circles, we often ask singles about when they'll be a couple, couples about when they'll get married, marrieds about when they'll have children, and so on. The church sets us on a path to family, so much so that we often trample over our own family members to get there. Many congregations build their entire liturgical infrastructure around a traditional family model: kids ministry, youth ministry, college ministry, premarital counselling, young marrieds groups, marriage conferences, family ministry, moms and dads groups, etc. There is a logic to this, as it largely defines people by the stage of life they're in.

But along the way, there are a myriad of individuals who aren't at just one age or just one stage. They also need family, crave community, thirst for inclusion, and are indirectly or directly being told that marriage is the primary means of accessing feelings of belonging.

So if they're going to remain single, it better be for a good reason.

This drive to make meaning out of one's relationship status can have a devastating impact on married people who expect their marriages to be the answer to all their emptiness. When it can't, they're left in a similar crisis of questioning their worth and value.

I witnessed a man in his fifties reflecting on the heartbreak of his divorce. He told me that the constant struggle to earn everything he needed to make his life perfect was actually what drove him and his wife apart. His story helped me see that the pursuit of family, if we're not careful, becomes a type of consumerism; we're never satisfied with what is and always pursuing the next thing. Our desire for connection can drive us to compete for the seemingly limited supply of suitable partners and view them as puzzle pieces that can complete our lives. As crass and unromantic as this characterization is, we perpetuate this economy of relational scarcity every time we envy another person's engagement announcement, covet their new baby, or wish that the attractive person on the airplane didn't have a ring on their finger. This

Darwinian mentality reduces our image of God to a lunchlady who rations cookies from her dessert cart. More for you means less for me.

A dangerous consequence of assuming there must be something useful about being single is that it's not a large leap for us to start trying to use God himself. Left unchecked, our prayer lives can start to sound more like bargaining from a person all too familiar with instant gratification: "Hey God, I'm delighting in you, now can I have what I asked for?"

When marriage isn't inevitable, singleness doesn't need to be useful.

LIE #3: SINGLENESS IS A TRAINING GROUND FOR MARRIAGE

She was more of an acquaintance than a friend, so it was already awkward. I knew very few people at her wedding reception. I bided my time with small talk until I could make a gracious exit during the bride and groom's first dance. However, the dance turned out to be captivating, and I was foolishly distracted from my escape plan. The bride's cultural tradition was for guests to pin money to her gown while she danced.

Before I could make a break for it, all the single women were called upon to catch the bouquet. The single men were to contend for the garter. How has this tradition survived into the twenty-first century?

It turned out that I knew more people at the reception than I realized, as they all began to point me out from my hiding place. They were motivated, because it turned out I was the only single woman in attendance. This spared me from exactly one indignity: having to demonstrate my lack of athleticism in acquiring the bouquet. Instead, all eyes stared me down in silence as the flowers were placed in my hands directly.

Around this time, I was apprised of another tradition in the bride's family: forcing the man who caught the garter and the woman who caught the bouquet to slow dance together in front of an entire room of strangers while they all smiled, laughed, and shouted, "You're next!"

In situations of extreme threat, the body will automatically select what it thinks will give you the best chance of survival. Typically, this involves one of four responses: fight, flight, freeze, flop. Apparently, psychologists had not yet discovered the fifth response: dancing with sweaty-palmed strangers while clinging to carnations.

Among the uses one often seeks out for singleness, preparation for marriage is the easiest to grab off the shelf. For far too long marriage was the lens through which I interpreted most of life's information. As long as marriage was the destination on my GPS, I could construe almost anything that happened to me as being part of the broken road that led me straight to marital bliss. I warped the concepts that God uses all things for our good (Romans 8:28) and orders my steps (Psalm 37:23) and somehow assumed them to mean that my present single state was setting me up for a better marital state. As long as marriage lingered as my ultimate ambition, everything else could be conceptualized as preparation for the future.

Many of us singles spend years preparing for marriage rather than learning how to be effective Christ-followers. This became most evident to me during a master's course I took on how to conduct couples therapy. In reviewing several therapeutic interventions for working with couples, I felt completely bored. That's when it occurred to this never-coupled woman in her thirties that I'd spent a lifetime learning how to be married. Some of this had been active learning through the books I read about praying for a husband or understanding men and women. Some of it was a byproduct of growing up with parents who had often provided marriage mentorship and counsel. But a lot of it was passive knowledge I'd picked up through sermons, Sunday school lessons, and youth conferences. In all that learning, I had never been taught how to be single, or to even consider doing singleness well in any way that wasn't connected to a future marriage.

I obviously learned some things on my own through my years of discovery—travel, entertainment, church hunting, changing careers, buying and selling cars, and moving between apartments and cities—but as I rehearsed the explicit instructions I'd picked up about how to communicate with a spouse, manage the division of household labour, navigate my sexuality, compromise, sacrifice, and talk about difficult things, I realized that most adult advice had come to me with a marital presumption. The church hadn't taught me how to be a person; it had taught me how to be a married person.

In trying to make sense of unwanted singleness, we often imply that singleness is no more than relationship prep school. We do this by identifying life lessons and events in relation to how they will best serve us in a marital state rather than by honouring them independently. Even if we don't intend it, we emphasize accomplishments that lead to romance more than we do other milestones.

One woman I know who married in her late forties confessed to me that although she had led an adventurous and accomplished life by most people's standards, she never felt so celebrated amongst her friends as when she got engaged. She was, of course, happy to be married and appreciated the joy of her friends, but she also found herself wondering whether her prior contributions to work, life, and humanity hadn't counted for much.

If you get married, you will naturally draw on your prior history of non-marriage and use those lessons and that wisdom to inform your future, but God is resourceful enough to make many meanings out of an experience—and marriage isn't the ultimate meaning. God's resourcefulness in using all the components of your life to redeem your brokenness and weave together disparate experiences and make them beautiful doesn't relegate every experience to a lesson. Your life is more a work of art than a gamified universe where certain tactical moves unlock the doors to other experiences. It's more of an integrated canvas than a linear process.

God has more for you. He expects more of you than to bide your time until marriage. When we don't assume that singleness is temporary, we are freed to ask deeper questions about our mission and purpose, to spend less time on preparation and more time on living a full life right now. When we realize that God is abundant in his resources, that he can help prepare us and make room for whatever comes our way, and that we don't have to save room for marriage, we fill our lives with love and service and meaning. A side benefit may be that we also release ourselves from the pressure to always be in spouse-recruitment mode and let our perfectionist mate-trapping veneers drop enough that we can venture to the grocery store in a hoodie and yoga pants without fear of missing our soulmate in the frozen food section.

I once lived in a boomtown known for its transience. While some people invested in it and made it a home, many were there with a highly consumeristic mindset. Those who relocated were typically on a one- to five-year exit strategy, and many lived as long-distance commuters who returned to their real lives and communities on days off.

I ran a young adults' ministry through a local church and had opportunities to observe both the positive and negative impacts of this mindset. On the plus side, people were inordinately friendly and inclusive. Each recognized how hard it was to move to a new place without connections, and how important it was to find people to do life with, so they formed an almost instant sense of community. It was rare for a new person our age to attend church without being invited to a meal, study, or event immediately after.

On the downside, people often treated this period as a temporary part of their lives, living according to a suitcase mentality. When you go somewhere and know you're only staying a short time, it's unlikely that you'll unpack much. Forget decorating or making the place feel like home! You may not even put clothing into drawers.

But if you end up staying longer, the very thing that made you feel comfortable before—the fact that this wasn't home—will make it unbearable long-term. I've known many people with this suitcase mentality.

"I'm only going to be in this stage for a while, so I won't bring all of who I am," they say to themselves. "It's too much work. It will hurt too much later."

This is why it can be such a trap to see singleness as temporary. You're far less likely to unpack, be vulnerable, and let the real you out to play. If you're only biding your time until a relationship comes along, if all you see in your current circumstances is what can be mined towards a different future, then singleness will feel increasingly uncomfortable.

Maybe it's time to unpack.

A single friend once shared with me that she desperately wanted God to just tell her once and for all whether she would ever get married.

"It would be easier to know," she moaned.

"What would you do if you knew?" I asked.

"I'd be able to finally just live my life and stop worrying about finding someone."

"Why don't you just do that now?"

It was a big pivot for me to stop thinking of my life as training and just start *living*. While pursuing a full, Christ-centred life might help me be a better partner should romance come along, I can attest that preparing for marriage didn't automatically help me live a good single life. This isn't about giving up on love; it's about giving up the bondage of an unguaranteed future.

When marriage isn't inevitable, singleness becomes its own life to be lived.

LIE #4: SINGLENESS IS SEASONAL

I started drinking coffee at the age of fourteen. I grew up in a home where coffee worship had been normalized, and I wanted to be just like the adults in my life. My early morning classes served as the perfect excuse to dabble with caffeine dependence. I didn't like it at first, but through many spoons of sugar and generous pours of cream, I acquired a taste for what would become a treasured daily ritual and lifeline throughout my education and early career.

After grad school, I developed a mild health condition that required me to stop drinking coffee. This was no easy feat. More than the caffeine withdrawal, I experienced the grief of losing a sacred liturgy. I mourned the smell of roasted beans first thing in the morning, the dark nutty flavour signalling alertness, the warmth of a mug hugged close to my chest as I sifted through my daily email, the excuse to get a break from the office and socialize with colleagues, the pretentiousness over roaster quality, the variety in selecting a precise combination of components to suit my mood that day—whether it be grande, dark roast, non-fat, extra hot, and so forth...

For weeks and weeks after quitting, I pined for coffee. If someone suggested I have tea instead, I pouted shamelessly and lamented that it wasn't the same. I kept hoping that after taking a short break from coffee I would be able to return to my routine. When people asked me if I was a coffee drinker, I still answered "Yes." As weeks turned into months, I continued to hope that the abstinence was a temporary inconvenience. In short order, I would welcome back the sweet nectar of the gods.

But that never happened.

It took me more than two years to admit that I was no longer a coffee drinker. After months of grappling with the void in my life, I realized that I had to figure out a way to fill the vacuum.

However begrudgingly, I acquired a taste for tea. I tried different brands, flavours, and types. I bought myself pretty teacups and toyed around with various steeping methods. I went to fancy restaurants that served tea in special china pots alongside three-tiered scallop-edged platters of scones, tarts, and cucumber sandwiches. I found out which teas I liked with accoutrements and which I preferred in their natural states. I stocked my kitchen and office with varieties of tea to serve various functions: morning wake-up teas, soothing feel-better teas, subtle evening teas, and sweet-tooth teas. Even my social media memes began to shift from coffee addict commentary to jokes and message mugs about being tea-crazed.

I gave up coffee in 2018. I still miss it, but it has become more bearable and even enjoyable since I've accepted reality. To embrace my identity as a tea drinker, I had to let go of the assumption that coffee would be part of my future.

Warm beverages may serve as a silly metaphor, but I truly believe that embracing singleness requires one to accept that coupledom isn't guaranteed. This is why I'm so cautious about using seasonal language to describe relationship status. I often hear people describe singleness as a season. I think this language comes from honest biblical intentions. It's true that this side of eternity is temporary, and that *"there is a time for everything, and a season for every activity under the heavens"* (Ecclesiastes 3:1). But I think relational seasons may be best labelled after they occur, not while they're in progress—or worse, before they happen (James 4:13–15). Even if you want to consider your present relational state as a season, it's pretty difficult to know how long that season will last.

Can you imagine discussing marriage in the same temporary language we do singleness? How strange would it be if, at the next wedding ceremony you attend, the minister skipped talking about how patient and kind love is (1 Corinthians 13:4) and instead told the couple to enjoy their season of marriage? How odd would it be for me to ask my coupled friends, after they did something independent like travel alone, "Why are you not divorced yet? How are you still married?" Yet we compare single people's present accomplishments to future relational states all the time.

While those who have since been divorced or widowed may look back on their time of marriage as a season, it's problematic to enter marriage that way. Seeing marriage as temporary lays the foundation for excuses to not do marriage well. I would argue that seeing singleness as temporary can have the same effect. By sloughing it off as short-term, we make excuses for not living well in our singleness. Many who manage their singleness miserably are perplexed as to why they are miserable, but the reality is that we reap from our singleness what we sow into it.

Sometimes seasonal language is a way for couples to try relating to singles by recalling their days before marriage. As with so many life stories, it's important to recognize that not every single experience is the same.

There is more than five years in age difference between me and my younger siblings. This means that I graduated from university when they were still in high school. While I had been to high school and had many memories and experiences to draw from, my siblings would get defensive when I tried to relate to them as one who fully understood their situation.

"Maybe you went to high school, but you're not in high school now," they would say.

They weren't wrong. Significant change had occurred in education and youth culture since I'd haunted the halls of a secondary school. While I have been a high school student and can reference some of that common experience, I can no longer say that I know what it's like to be in high school. Even if my siblings later graduated and realized I knew more than they gave me credit for, there was a chasm that my experience couldn't cross.

I think the same is true when those who are coupled try to connect with singles. Of course, they were single and could give insight. It's not as if all wisdom and memory are erased at the altar. But there is a significant difference between recall and present experience. Just because you knew what it *was* like doesn't mean you know what it *is* like.

Singleness is its own state and has its own rules whether it precedes a relationship or not. God is guiding and empowering my life on the earth to prepare me for a life in eternity, not to make sure I have the most romantic existence possible. Of course he cares about family, marriage, love, and commitment, but he also cares about character, mission, inspiration, and creative process. He cares about our relationships because he cares about us. Unlike a Hollywood screenwriter, though, his ultimate goal isn't to have everyone happily coupled off by the end of the movie.

When marriage isn't inevitable, singleness can be treated legitimately and uniquely.

LIE #5: YOU'RE JUST NOT READY

Assuming that marriage is inevitable and singleness requires an explanation neglects the truth that romance and relationships are developed on a murky continuum of trial, error, and courage and ignores the thousands of possible paths that are available to those not fixated on only one aspect of human experience. It also fuels the harmful idea that a person's relationship status is a reward they earn through being ready, and conversely that singleness is some kind of purgatory for those who have yet to achieve this readiness.

This sets up single people to embrace faulty thinking on either end of the spectrum. On one end, if marriage is the ultimate reward, we're likely to do anything to attain it regardless of morals, values, relational compatibility, or discernment. On the other end, if it's all about being ready, we're likely to evaluate people legalistically through the filter of romantic suitability.

Insisting on a destination of romantic love forces us to scrutinize people in a way we otherwise wouldn't. I sometimes wonder whether we don't consider marriage an ultimate goal because it gives our craving for legalism a hit by granting us permission to demand perfection of ourselves and others. It provides us with a false sense of control over causes and effects, actions and results, behaviours and rewards.

When we think in terms of readiness, not only do we have an invisible measuring stick for ourselves, but we hold one out to others, negating their humanity in a quest for romantic suitability. While we can make this seem rational, it's usually done in the context of a vaguely defined idea of readiness that's undermined as soon as a couple demonstrates less maturity, growth, or development in an area we previously thought to be a lynchpin criterion. In other words, a nineteen-year-old who gets married tomorrow doesn't do so by being more "ready" than a forty-year-old single person.

This readiness concept is a natural result of us working to make sense of an uncomfortable world and demonstrates that we often distance ourselves out of self-protection. When we can't explain our singleness, or even fear it, we may feel better to assume something we've done or haven't done will prevent it from happening to us. I know that I've been spiritually convicted of looking to older single women and mentally itemizing all the reasons I think they might be single, reasons that don't apply to me, out of a sense of relational superiority. It's a falsely comforting thought to conclude that we won't be single at that age because we don't behave in a certain way.

Obviously, compatibility, communication, commitment, and many other aspects of marriage will benefit from a couple's maturity, self-awareness, and life experience. But it's easy for this to also serve less constructive functions—as an excuse for not taking romantic or commitment risks ("I'm not ready yet"), as the commodification of marriage ("I earned this"), as a way of othering single people ("They're not ready"), and thereby disqualifying an entire category of adults ("When they get their act together, they can join our club").

But relationships aren't achievements. They are choices. We don't earn a marriage. And when we assume that one must be ready for marriage, we also assume that one must get married at all.

There's another connected and damaging narrative that has arisen from both the lie of readiness and the lie of seeing singleness as a training ground for relationships. How often are singles instructed to work on themselves in order to find a partner? I've heard this from so many pulpits and podiums. Speakers constantly address the value of reflection, healing, therapy, and spiritual discipline, and then dangle the carrot of a relationship as an incentive. It's as though they're saying, "If you delight in the Lord, you'll probably find a spouse." This diminishes singleness, relationships, and sanctification all at once.

Marriage is not a reward for good single behaviour.

In most cases, I think we would do better to reexamine our definitions of adulthood rather than our concepts of marital readiness. Marriage may be a process that grows you up, but the act of a wedding does not magically bestow maturity onto people. Two immature people don't make one mature marriage. Besides which, in a culture increasingly familiar with prolonged adolescence, marriage and childrearing can no longer be considered the de facto litmus tests for affirmation of adulthood. Quite frankly, if marriage and parenting are all there is to adulthood, then I get why so many people opt out of growing up. In reality, we vary in our preparedness to take on the responsibility of adulthood, not just coupled adulthood.

Perhaps it's time to consider how we define and demarcate adulthood rather than treating singles as if they're not grown up or not ready. Examples of other recognition-worthy transitions from youth to maturity might include graduation, commencement of a career, gaining an independent dwelling (or successful community dwelling), travelling internationally, contracting professionals like lawyers, agents, or bankers, and volunteering or working in roles with increasing responsibility and leadership. This would open the doors of inclusivity to allow all adults, regardless of relationship status, to engage and find community around things they have in common outside of family.

Can you imagine a church where men and women could relate to one another around their professions, hobbies, and personal struggles instead of just their kids and marriages? Let's stop equating marriage with maturity.

And of course, none of these discussions so far have addressed the quality or permanence of modern romantic partnerships. Narratives that fixate on just finding a relationship often neglect to comment on whether that relationship is compatible, harmonious, or enduring. It's as if the mere act of acquiring a relationship is enough to satisfy our idea of maturity, regardless of how things proceed from there.

If we are to invoke a philosophy of readiness, let us at least take it all the way to its logical end and give it a chance to actually serve us. Being single is work. Being married is work. Loving others is work. Following Christ is work. Being an adult is work.

Ready or not, here it comes.

DETHRONING THE MARRIAGE IDOL

There's nothing wrong with desiring a spouse, and I still do, but it is always problematic when we make good things the *ultimate* things.[5] It's far too easy to make an idol out of romantic partnership or assume that romantic love is superior. It doesn't take much mental energy to cast coupledom as the answer to singleness. Perhaps if we weren't so busy glorifying marriage, we could have more honest conversations about the beauties and challenges of adulthood more broadly and how we can glorify God.

The thing about hoping in something, desiring something, or even worshipping something is that the fixation changes us. It's difficult not to mimic what we devote our attention to or become what we behold. This doesn't mean that we'll become married if we desire marriage strongly enough, but we will become more like someone who wants to be married than someone who wants to be like Jesus. We'll become more convinced that marriage is the ultimate pursuit, more prone to see everything else God has for us as impeding that goal, and increasingly resentful of both the desire for marriage itself and the one we think gave it to us.

I've been spiritually convicted for having put my hope in a future marriage rather than in God. Misplaced hope for romance, I've realized, has been more of a burden to me than my actual singleness. While it's easy to justify how I've idolized marriage, it's now my responsibility to dethrone it and allow God to take his rightful place.

If you're modelling your life after a figure that looks more like Cinderella than Christ, you might be bowing to a marriage idol. If every prayer you pray and every plan you make circles around the idea of a future relationship, you might be bowing to a marriage idol. If you assume that your friend's singleness is temporary and are waiting for them to find a partner in order to relate to them, you might be bowing to a marriage idol. If you're inside a marriage secretly wondering why your spouse isn't fulfilling you, you might be bowing to a marriage idol. If you consider the trend towards singleness as a threat to the family, you might be bowing to a marriage idol. If you've confused the love of God for a far lesser romantic human love, you might be bowing to a marriage idol.

As with all idols, its worship is selfish, exhausting, and unsatisfying.

It's time for us as the church to unhook the gospel from the American dream. For too long we have equated salvation with romance, and holiness with family. The people around us will ask us questions based on what we centre our lives around as Christians. I'm okay if the way I live provokes people to ask for an explanation for my life, but I want it to be for my hope in Jesus, not my hope in marriage. When we think about what's beyond marriage, we stumble onto a whole new realm of God's goodness and provision, regardless of our relationship status.

As I've released my hold on the future I thought I wanted, I've been permitted to ponder the wonder of a recklessly loving question: what if God has more for me than marriage?

PART TWO

RECKON WITH
Desire

PART TWO

THE ELEPHANT IN THE ROOM

*Courage is the most important of all the virtues
because without courage, you can't practice any
other virtue consistently.*[6]
—Maya Angelou

SEX. WE CAN'T not talk about it. It's too big of an issue. And yes, we might be able to reduce the pressure of this topic if more people embraced the idea that marriage isn't inevitable, but I think sex and singleness would still demand our attention. So many of us understand sex differently that it can be hard to name it and give it an appropriate place in any conversation.

In coming to grips with our single status, we may talk about grieving a married life. We may mourn that we'll never experience romance. At some point, though, we'll have to own up to the fact that asking about whether we'll ever get married is at least partially a guise for a different question, the elephant in the room of Christian singleness: "Will I ever get to have sex?" Or to put it a different way, "Will I ever get to have God-approved sex?"

To address the question of singleness in Christian circles, we have to discuss celibacy. Many writers explain why Christian singles should remain celibate. I would guess that, like me, you've read some of them, if not many.

However, there are probably more writers that teach the opposite—that celibacy is antiquated, the church should butt out of the bedroom, and people should have as much consenting sex as they want with whomever they choose. I'm not going to rehash either of those arguments because I think they miss something I would much rather explore: *how* are we to be celibate? And for those interested in pursuing an abstinent lifestyle, what actual strategies can they employ?

Let me provide a giant disclaimer before we dive in. I'm a Christian Caucasian heterosexual woman and extremely grateful that so far in my life I've not experienced sexualized violence directly. This informs the perspective from which I approach the subject. However, it doesn't mean there is any sexual practice that can put anyone outside of God's love or redemptive path. I think that having to justify singleness often leads to extreme forms of judgmentalism, stigmatization, prejudice, assumption, and scapegoating of sexuality that is uncalled for.

Furthermore, I don't think you have to be celibate to learn about celibacy, or to benefit from the non-sex-related portions of this book, nor do I think you have to be sexually active to learn about sex. I think we could all benefit from a more nuanced understanding of sex than is possible when we treat it as an abstraction—or worse, a filthy word not to be spoken of.

Let me also add that while I research, explore, and continue to form opinions in my best effort to treat this subject in an authentic and scripture-informed way, I know that I'm not always right. I am keenly aware of how much damage has been written into this space and am hopeful to unpack that damage rather than add to it.

My prayer is that the following words bring life, that they increase grace and courage, and that all who read them may move towards freedom and wholeness wherever they find themselves.

I will shortly take issue with the language of "waiting" when it comes to discussing sexuality. But because I know the word has broad familiarity, let me say this: to those who have waited, to those who have not waited, to those who wish they had waited, to those whose choice to wait was stolen, to those who have always waited, and to those who are waiting now, read these next chapters knowing that it isn't about perfection, being irredeemable, or judgment. It's simply about the *how* of abstinence and the complexity of desire that are all too often ignored.

Five

WHY THIS CHRISTIAN SINGLE IS DONE WITH SAVING SEX

The glory of God is man fully alive.[7]
—Irenaeus

BY VIRTUE OF being single, I am largely underrepresented when it comes to an evangelical approach to sexuality. As one who grew up in church, I can't count the number of times I've heard it announced that it's time to do *that series* again: one based on sex or marriage or love or commitment. It's usually announced in late winter to most inconveniently coincide with Valentine's Day. The series is always meant for married people, because marriage is what makes it okay for us Christians to talk about sex.

But rather than acknowledge that not everyone is in the same stage of life and that some messages won't apply to the whole room—which is okay and part of learning from a greater community—there is always at least part of one message explicitly reserved "for the singles." This is usually preached by a married male pastor who met his current wife of twenty-plus years when they were both seventeen or in Bible college.

The message can be summed up in one word: *wait!* Although it might be said in other ways.

"Sex isn't for you—yet."

"Pray for a spouse."

"If you've already had sex, God will forgive you."

"Porn is destructive."

"Masturbation is selfish."

"Imagine the gift you will be for someone one day!"

Seldom discussed are matters of rape, consent, and abuse or issues of gender, though those conversations dominate our media feeds nearly every day. Some brave pulpiteers may broach the subjects of sexual orientation, affairs, and that all-encompassing word for anything uncomfortably sexual, *lust*.

Regardless, this message isn't targeted at the one demographic that statistics reveal to be growing in the church and the world: singles without marriage on the horizon.

In the church, you're either married or not-yet-married—unless of course you have the elusive gift of celibacy, which few seem to think they possess. This idea comes from the apostle Paul, who wrote that we are better off staying single and serving the Lord full-time. According to Paul, if we can't stay celibate, *"it is better to marry than to burn with passion"* (1 Corinthians 7:9). For years, on account of this one verse, Christians have tried to tie abstinence in a bow without discussing what's inside the package. Instead any ounce of sexual desire is understood to be a disqualification for the gift rather than a part of managing it.

To sum up, people who aren't horny are made to feel like they should be nuns and priests, and people who are horny end up feeling like they have a spiritual justification for not having to spend another second of their lives unwed. Many give up altogether and walk away from their faith over this issue, or at the very least they decide that conservative sexual ethics are antiquated and must no longer apply.

It's not that I personally take issue with a Christian approach to sex being reserved for marriage. But I have a problem with the idea that sex is to be *saved* for marriage. A huge problem!

For years and years of witch burning and scarlet lettering, chastity rings, teen purity conferences, commitment ceremonies, and courtship weekends, Christianity has been branding virginity as an effort to save oneself for marriage. It's the ultimate gift you can give a spouse someday.

Such preservation conjures up imagery of currency where sex is something to be saved up and spent on a future spouse; other expenditures diminish the total gift to be allotted. It may also invoke the idea of a piggy bank that may eventually burst if you don't find something on which to spend the accumulating coins.

That's all fine and well if you end up getting married, but what if you don't? What are you going to do with all that money burning a hole in your pocket? If you have money in your sex bank, you should spend it on marriage; if you don't have money in your sex bank, it's because you're destined for monastic living.

That leaves the rest of us in a third category that remains unaddressed in any church I've ever attended: those who have money in their sex bank and have nothing to spend it on!

The assumption that marriage is inevitable has a key flaw. Many singles today face the reality that marriage may never happen for them, or it may happen at a life stage well beyond one's sexual prime.

For others, marriage may have already happened and since ended.

So what are you saving sex for if you never get married, or feel like you never will? What are you saving it for if you've already been married but are now widowed or divorced and accruing sex currency at an alarming rate? What are you saving it for now if you already spent a lot of it on past relationships? What's the point of engaging in a purity discussion if one doesn't have a future spousal relationship?

The other issue of course is that the idea of marriage has changed, whether the church likes it or not. Society is no longer upholding Christian tradition as their moral compass—and if they don't believe in or follow Jesus, why would they? Different denominations don't even agree on how marriage should be defined. While the evangelical church continues to interpret heterosexual monogamous commitment as the basis for marriage, it's naïve to assume this is still the standard definition. In a country that legally acknowledges marital rights for common-law and homosexual couples, the concept of saving sex for marriage has quite literally lost its meaning. It's no longer self-explanatory in an evangelical setting.

Those of my generation who grew up in church likely heard the same purity messages about how to avoid leading on those of the opposite sex, how to shut down physical interaction before things get too heated, how hormones betray us, and how to save up all our sexual sensations for a future spouse. Our heads were filled with the dos and don'ts of sexual interaction in order to set ourselves up for a healthy heterosexual marriage.

None of this prepared us for not-marriage, or for homosexual attraction, or for porn, or other issues and arousals we didn't expect. Dogma only told us where to set boundaries within and in preparation for one specific type of relationship.

By dealing so specifically with some sexual issues and not others, we eliminate discussions of how to respond to what society lobs at us. When our approach to sex is narrow, we lose the big picture. Purity isn't about our connection to a sacred text, relationships with other people, or even the relationship with ourselves, though that is too often overlooked; it's first and foremost about our relationship with God.

Sex inside marriage is God's design, but saving yourself for marriage is bad theology. It fails to acknowledge that impurity is destructive whether you ever get married. It can also lead to the deceptive promise that sex within monogamy is perfect (it's not), or that sex outside marriage cannot be forgiven or redeemed (it can). By saving myself for marriage, I'm constantly defined by a future version of myself as a spouse. Therefore, a large part of my identity consists of who I am or am not engaging with sexually. Those of us who actually maintain our abstinence are shamed no matter where we turn. To the world, we're prudes; to the church, we're incomplete.

Perhaps the most damaging and heartbreaking facet of the save-sex-for-marriage theology is that when sexual urges, desires and frustrations emerge in the life of a single person—and they will—God is immediately cast as the withholder who's robbing us of the gifts of marriage and sex, rather than as the good, gift-giving Father (Matthew 7:11) who desires our abundant life (John 10:10). How do we expect to bring good news to a world obsessed with, and conflicted about, sexual identity if we can't find our own identities outside our sex lives?

God has a much bigger definition of you than who you choose to sleep with. A theology where all sexual behaviour is brought into the context of honouring God is far more freeing, thorough, and inclusive. It allows us to explore a purpose beyond our sexual proclivities.

Sex isn't being stored up in you, although it can feel that way, nor is it a genetic need, though we often speak as if it is. While biological and

God-given, sex does not fall into the same category as food, water, or shelter. Sex is a gift, but celibacy is also a gift from God to you, from you to him, and from you to yourself. We aren't waiting for marriage or waiting for sex; we wait for the Lord and his plan, whatever it may be (Psalm 27:14).

I'm not saving myself for marriage. I'm trying to live fully in my singleness for my God.

MANAGING A NON-SEX LIFE

It is the nature of desire not to be satisfied, and most human beings live only for the gratification of it.[8]
—Aristotle

SO HOW DO I manage sexuality and purity in a state of singleness? This is the question I started asking in my twenties. In the early days, I summoned my courage and tentatively approached older Christian women who were either still single or had married later in life, trying to suss out in the politest way possible whether they had managed to keep their pants on—and if so, how they managed it. What did they do on those evenings when they were turned on by a love scene in a movie or the vibrations from their cell phone? How did they not bemoan every hand-holding couple in the park? Were they angry at God for not bringing them a sexual partner? Were they bitter at the world for constantly berating them with advice about casual sex, or at the church for treating them like children?

Was there a solution for me somewhere between the two poles of "screw abstinence" (pun intended) and "marry immediately"?

Breaking free of the dominant Christian sexual narrative was only half the battle. Discovering new ways of thinking about sex, celibacy, longing, and intimacy, and in the process finding pure ways to embrace sexuality, have been ongoing struggles.

I remember sitting across from a very unsingle lead pastor, explaining to him that his latest message about relationships had failed to reach the single demographic in his church, since it had conformed to the trope of assuming one would be married eventually. Growing up as a pastor's kid, I knew better than to assume that pastors have all the answers, but I was still surprised to observe him taking notes as I spoke.

"I've never heard a pastor speak about how to actually manage sexual desire," I said. "They usually just chastise me to control it."

As I braced myself for the barrage of scripture verses that were no doubt about to come my way, I met his inquisitive stare.

"So how do you manage it?" he asked expectantly, pen poised to document my answer.

The revelation was stunning in its simplicity. I choked back a gasp as I realized what should have been obvious: they don't talk about how to do this because they don't know.

Nobody knows.

As with so many areas of life that aren't explicitly marked out for us in scripture, somewhere between do and don't is the beauty, mystery, and frustration of listening to and communing with the Holy Spirit for answers. For me, these answers have included mind shifts and practical steps from a variety of sources. I'm still exploring them.

I don't know how God wants you to manage your sex life. Perhaps you might think of it as a non-sex life! But I can share with you how he is helping me to manage mine.

THE GIFT NOBODY WANTS

> I wish that all of you were as I am. But each of you has your own gift from God; one has this gift, another has that.
>
> Now to the unmarried and the widows I say: It is good for them to stay unmarried, as I do. But if they cannot control themselves, they should marry, for it is better to marry than to burn with passion. (1 Corinthians 7:7–9)

The misinterpretation of this passage and fundamental misunderstanding of the gift of singleness has led to much angst in the church. Note that I'll use the terms *single* and *celibate* interchangeably in this chapter, as I think they're understood to be the same in this context. If it's better to marry than to burn with passion, some may think that they must not have the gift of singleness. "I want to have sex; therefore, I don't have the gift." According to this interpretation, any experience of sexual energy is a signal that singleness is not part of God's plan for a person's life.

These verses are actually given in the context of a mini-lecture by Paul on sexual immorality and the appropriate Christian response to lust and sexual desire, which is sacrifice, worship, and remembering that our bodies are temples of the Holy Spirit (1 Corinthians 6:19). He essentially says that he is pro-celibacy, but if people are going to engage sexually they should at least do so in the context of marriage.

Paul saw celibacy as an act of worship and way to connect intimately with God. He didn't call it a gift sarcastically or offer the option of singleness apologetically. In fact, this may be the most explicitly pro-single passage of scripture in the Bible.

As a formerly devout Jew, steeped in the family tradition of his day, Paul had a direct encounter with Jesus and transformed from being a Christ denier to a martyr for the faith. He authored much of the New Testament as an early father of the Christian faith. And here he tells believers that he thinks singleness is preferable to marriage!

Why do we find that so uncomfortable? Why do we immediately breeze past this and move on to the Paul's advice for marriage? What is so important about marriage that we hold it supreme?

It perplexes me that this passage, which clearly holds up singleness as being preferable to marriage, is so often used to dismiss the celibate. If we allow ourselves to stop dismissing Paul as an eccentric, we may just see the beauty and function of celibacy.

Singles are often told that they're either married and godly or single and sinful. But if we must find cruelty in this passage, the more obvious choice would be to decide that marriage is less a reward for the abstinent and more a contingency plan for those who lack self-control.

Regardless, both singleness and marriage are framed as gifts. So why under the Christmas tree of life do we cast coupledom as the shiny package and singleness as the itchy sweater from an eccentric aunt? Is marriage more God's plan than celibacy? The short answer is no.

The long answer is that the short answer is hard for most people to accept.

Jesus understood this. In Matthew 19, after realizing how highly he upheld marriage as a holy union and yet how seriously he considered divorce, the disciples asked Jesus if perhaps it was better not to marry at all. Jesus acknowledged that accepting such a truth was difficult, and not everyone could make room in their hearts and minds for the concept of abstinence, whether chosen or inflicted (Matthew 19:10–12).

This tells me that addressing celibacy requires that we seek to embrace it. We need to make room in our hearts and minds to receive a more hopeful message about how it can be a blessing to us and the kingdom of God.

Many of us have come to see celibacy as an inferior option to having an active sex life. At least many of us reside in social contexts where it's framed this way. It may be one reason why we're so eager to consider singleness in temporary terms, because we don't want to inflict the destiny of celibacy on others. I've heard pastors bemoan the advice they must give those who fall short of their interpretation of the scriptural permissibility for marriage, as if it removes all hope. If we see the hope of marriage as less cruel than the guarantee of celibacy, what does that say about our approach to sexuality and spirituality? As a Christ-follower, I am called to the straight and narrow (Matthew 17:13–14), but I am also invited to a banquet table (Matthew 22:2–14). If we keep casting marriage as the banquet table, and singleness as the scraps on the floor, we're always going to struggle to offer single people hope.

When I'm honest with myself and open with others, I can see that my life is in many ways much more expansive because of my celibacy. Where I once thought God might be restricting me, I now realize that he has actually opened so many doors. As a person with whom many people share their problems, I've been amazed to discover how much drama and emotional turmoil sex can exact on a person. It's surprising how many people expect full satisfaction to be found in sex, and how steep the disappointment is when they can't find it. I have come to want more out of life than a sex life, yet I often feel that the church judges me for being incomplete more than the rest of the world does. Secular society now considers asexuality to be a valid identity, for example.

I believe that the church needs to wake up to its pervasive hypocrisy. We can't continue to promote abstinence and virginity as the moral high ground and then treat celibacy as second-best. If we want to share the love and freedom of Jesus, and if we ever want singles to find true community in our midst, we must not shame them. Wouldn't it be amazing to have a vision for people, for sexuality, where it didn't feel like encouraging God's best was akin to some kind of punishment?

If you're single, it's a gift from God to you. The word gift in Paul's letter is translated from the same Greek word from which we get *charisma*.[9] Charisma is defined as favour freely given and a gift of grace. It's the same word used in this frequently quoted passage: *"For the wages of sin is death, but the gift of God is eternal life..."* (Romans 6:23) It's the same word used later in 1 Corinthians when Paul describes the gifts of the spirit (1 Corinthians 12). This gift comes from and is empowered by God.

We often miss the detail that we have a role to play in the discipline of managing, developing, and growing that gift. Perhaps we fail to recognize the gift of singleness because we have neglected the skills that support the gift.

I am by nature a very musical person. I was singing before I spoke, writing songs before I knew how to spell, and playing around with musical instruments before my hands were big enough to span their many keys. To a very real extent, I was born with a God-given gift. But that gift for music would have waned if I had done nothing with it. I had to take lessons to hone it, practicing, auditioning, and performing. I have revelled in the euphoria of seeing music transform and suffered injury at the cost of producing it, including succumbing to carpal tunnel, tinnitus, calloused hands, sore lips, and strained vocal cords, not to mention the emotional toll of countless audition rejections.

Had I not developed the skills of musicality, or the resilience of pursuing a craft, one might not even know I had the gift of music.

When we don't feel gifted, or when we don't like the gift, we may mistakenly conclude we don't have the gift. When it comes to singleness, we waste energy seeking the traits in us that disqualify us rather than the traits in singleness that could make our lives more meaningful. God offers us an inheritance of abundance, and we protest with semantics and legalities that would see the testament of his wishes fall to others. As with any inheritance, it can seem like a mixed bag at first. Yes, there are obvious treasures. But there are many less obvious artifacts that require attention before we uncover their worth and meaning. We may have to take the time to discover the true value of the inheritance we have been given.

We must make an important distinction between the concepts of a gift and a calling. I think many people assume that the gift of singleness comes after some divine moment of heavenly direction that bequeaths us with superpowers: "Thou shalt be single!" And if we haven't heard that call, we must not have the gift.

I don't think it works that way.

Even though marriage is also framed as a gift, we have few discussions about whether one is gifted or called to marriage, or whether one has the capacity to accept Jesus's teaching on the subject. The logic is further flawed when we remember that singleness is actually our default state; marriage is one we must opt into. What would the world look like if we assumed we were all to be single unless we heard a divine call to marriage?

I seldom, if ever, hear of single people looking for the reasons why they might not have the gift of marriage. I've heard people pray to receive the gift of marriage, but no one seems to pray for the gift of celibacy, to remove the desire for marriage and increase the desire for singleness.

What would it look like if we confidently and faithfully asked God to provide the space and wisdom to steward celibacy?

Does stewarding the gift of singleness mean that we never pursue romance or marriage? Probably not. However, seeking marriage can distract us from the gifts God has for us in our singleness, and not finding someone to marry can quickly become an excuse for mismanaging sexual desire. The skills of celibacy management apply even to those who do get married, both for seasons when sex isn't possible and for the renewed singleness that occurs after the loss of one's spouse. Focusing on how to value the gift of singleness can also make a person a lot busier, which can be an excellent antidote for the single who isn't so much desirous, or even lonely, as they are bored.

Scripture, literature, history, and modern life are rife with stories about gifts that come in unexpected packages, blessings that showed up as potential problems, and circumstances requiring faith that didn't make sense until much later in the narrative. I'm doubtful that King David's run as a shepherd boy, having to ward off lions and bears, always felt like a gift to him. But I'm guessing all that experience felt rather divine once he had defeated Goliath. The time he spent running from the ego-threatened Saul was likely the boot camp he needed in order to handle the pressures of kinghood (1 Samuel 17).

Similarly, Esther's time in a harem, isolated from her family, helped to fashion her queenship and strengthened her tenacity in defending her people to a powerful king (Esther 1–10).

But according to pastor and podcaster Erwin McManus, "The greatest gift God can give you will feel like a curse if you want the wrong thing."[10] Even if you see singleness as the thorn in your side (2 Corinthians 12:7) rather than a gift, it's still incumbent on you to use that thorn to draw closer to God, wrestle with his will (Genesis 32:22–32), and find ways to praise him in spite of it.

How do you know you have the gift of singleness? You know it if you're single.

Sometimes I think we're scared to receive God's gift of singleness, because we fear he may not give us other gifts, like marriage, if we accept it. God is far more abundant than this scarcity mindset. The fear reveals that our perspective on celibacy and singleness is less about us and more about how little we trust God. The question isn't "Is this a gift?" or even "Is this my gift?" The question is "Do I trust the gift-giver?"

For as long as I am single, I have the gift of singleness.

SEX IS ALWAYS AN ISSUE

I remember one of the conversations I was brave enough to start with a woman who married a bit later in life. She shared with me how she had thought managing her sex drive and impulses would be solved by marriage, only to be almost comically corrected. Due to some complicated biology that had to be resolved surgically, she and her husband weren't able to properly consummate until eighteen months into their marriage.

After disclosing this, she dropped the truth bomb: sex will never not be an issue.

We're sometimes taught to resist the myth of perfect sex when it shows up in media, having been warned about Hollywood's many unrealistic sexual encounters, but we may be less shielded from sexual glorification within church buildings, such as when youth pastors talk about their hot wives or pastors outline the erotic imagery of the Song of Solomon. In church, marriage is treated as the epitome of adulthood, and sex is often portrayed as the thing that completes us.

Because of how it's depicted both inside and outside the church, it's easy to assume that finally getting to have Christ-approved sex will solve all the sexual problems of singleness. What isn't announced so loudly is the truth that compatibility takes time, that we may have to sort out physiological and anatomical issues, that partners won't always be in the mood at the same time, and that pregnancy, birth, childrearing, illness, surgery, travel, body image issues, and any number of other factors will impact people at different times. Even the longest night of rapture is still a fleeting moment in the context of a relationship, and shorter still in the context of life. Whether during singleness or outside it, we must reckon with and sacrifice our sexual desires. Letting go of a sexual ideal can make abstinence more bearable, and doing the work to understand our sexual selves will always have value.

I've found it helpful to gain clarity on what sexual desire is and what it isn't. Andy Stanley teaches that desire is like an appetite.[11] Appetites are never satisfied. The lie of the appetite is always the same: "If I feed it, it will go away." This lie tricks me into thinking that I won't have to manage the appetite if I give in to it. This isn't true of any appetite.

Take an appetite for food. If you're hungry and never eat, you have to manage your appetite. And if you eat, you have to manage your appetite in a state of indulgence by choosing and preparing food, monitoring your portions, and dealing with the impact of over or undereating.

With sex, you have to manage wanting to act on your desire. But if you give in to that desire, you still have to manage the appetite. With whom will you satisfy it? Does it mean more to one than the other? Do you have mutual consent? What happens if someone gets pregnant? What happens if someone contracts a disease? What happens if the sex isn't good? And so on.

Mimicking the voice of the appetite, the Enemy beckons, "Come here. Give in. Resolve the tension." But the truth is that you're just picking your tension. The appetite has to be managed in both indulgence and abstention.

Sin obviously has a role in this, but the role isn't as big as we make it out to be. I often hear about the sin of temptation when it comes to sex. I think this is a way in which we give the Enemy unnecessary credit.

First of all, temptation is not a sin, for even Jesus was tempted (Matthew 4:1–11); acting on it is. Actively seducing someone may be sinful, but that is different than being tempted yourself.

Secondly, while lust is a sin and one way of feeding a sexual appetite, a sexual appetite isn't inherently sinful. In fact, the appetite may just be a sign of what Solomon calls God setting *"eternity in the human heart"* (Ecclesiastes 3:11). In other words, the reason you can never satisfy your appetites is because you can never get enough of life!

When sin touches an appetite, it can pervert or twist it into an addiction, but the God-given appetite itself is a deeply visceral experience of things to come. In this way, sexual desire is a sign of eternity that the celibate get to experience in a unique way.

For me, it's been pretty important not to interpret sexual desire as a need. If you subscribe to the view that sex is reserved for marriage, that also means that you don't actually need sex until marriage. One reason that sex is reserved for marriage is because God intends it as a tool for expressing intimacy in a unique way with one's spouse. Sex is thought to unite two people in an unbreakable bond. According to this theology, any other use of sex is the incorrect application of a very specific tool, which is a foundation for disaster.

In one context, sex can be useful. In another, it can be destructive.

If I limit the definition of sex to just one of my primal instincts—natural, chemical, hormonal—and part of my physical make-up that I can't control, then my abstinence seems foolish. It feels like constant self-denial. In a lot of ways, abstinence actually is constant self-denial, but the shift in thinking is important; as long as I keep sex in the category of a need, rather than a desire, I continue to justify my want of it to God. He placed this need in me and he isn't fulfilling it.

Whether sex or not-sex, it isn't easy for anyone. The truth is that you aren't alone in the struggle. Other sexually inactive people may have insights as to how they manage their abstinence. If you're not getting help from someone, or can't find celibate friends, try gently asking advice of those who are widowed, divorced, or married to someone who's unable to have sex for any amount of time, for reasons such as illness, distance, absence, or travel. I'm sure you'll uncover helpful strategies.

WHY PURITY?

Purity is one way in which we respond to our appetites. When we subscribe to the save-sex-for-marriage doctrine, we establish that the motivation for virginal living is marriage, and by extension a great sex life. In doing this, we often vilify impurity as a potential threat against marriage. While possibly true, this is problematic not only because it assumes a future marriage but because trying to motivate holy living out of fear is to incentivize purity by threatening harm (Colossians 2:21–23).

Though it can be effective in the short-term, fear doesn't sustain morality in the long-term. You can't stay the same amount of scared of the same amount of stuff. Either the fear dissipates and you return to your initial behaviour or the threat grows larger in your mind to remain effective.

Take a rather benign example, such as the fear of spiders. When a spider enters a room, a person may react initially in fear, but given enough time they can usually regain enough composure to realize they're physically superior and can easily render the arachnid defenceless. If not, they'll build a perception that the spider is much larger, more conniving, and more frightening than it actually is.

All of this is to say that being scared that impurity will ruin a marriage isn't enough to keep me from being impure.

When we get the reward and motivation wrong, we get frustrated and stall over the question of why we shouldn't engage in sex if we won't ever marry. But the actual issue isn't sex or gratification. It's purity, which doesn't stop when you get married. Neither are the blessings of God somehow nonexistent until you do.

When you're single, one of the ways you steward and implement purity is through abstinence. And if you marry, one of the ways you steward and implement purity is through sex with your spouse. But sex isn't a reward for purity. The scriptures make it clear that the reward for purity is clarity about the will of God for your life.

> Blessed are the pure in heart, for they shall see God. (Matthew 5:8)

> Therefore, I urge you, brothers and sisters, in view of God's mercy, to offer your bodies as a living sacrifice, holy and pleasing to God—this is your true and proper worship. Do not conform to the pattern of this world, but be transformed by the renewing of your mind. Then you will be able to test and approve what God's will is—his good, pleasing and perfect will. (Romans 12:1–2)

> ...without holiness no one will see the Lord. (Hebrews 12:14)

There is a direct link between how I foster purity and how I hear from God and see his will play out in my life. Similarly, there is a correlation between surrendering to temptation and being knocked off life's course.

I've been the sharpest and clearest in my mission when I focused on the things of God. While God has never withdrawn from me, I can see that knowingly indulging in impurity always leads to the dulling of my spiritual senses. I become less peaceful, less able to rest and sleep, less intuitive, less clear-minded, and less confident. It's as if my ears have a little more wax in them, my skin a little more calloused and deadened to subtle touch. God isn't more or less present; I am more or less sensitive to his presence.

The link between acts of purity and connection with God is age-old. Through Abraham, God's people were commanded to circumcise themselves as a sign of his covenant with them (Genesis 17:11). Under a new covenant, this action is not required, but rather we show that we're God's people through devotion, or circumcision, of the heart (Romans 2:29). This symbolism can be taken uncomfortably far when you consider how Jesus spoke about eunuchs:

> For there are eunuchs who were born that way, and there are eunuchs who have been made eunuchs by others—and there are those who choose to live like eunuchs for the sake of the kingdom of heaven. (Matthew 19:12)

Celibacy is like being a eunuch of the heart, one who forfeits sexual activity out of devotion to God. This isn't done to earn his favour; it's a sign that his favour is already present. We acknowledge that his presence in our lives is more valuable than anything that could detract from it.

Even the purest person on earth will struggle with doubt and questions about God's will, but one path to confusion about God's direction is to mess with your management of purity. This is true whether you're single or not.

Regardless of your relationship status, the stewardship of your purity serves three functions:

1. It's an act of worship and obedience to God.
2. It's an act of self-respect.
3. It's a gift to fellow believers in that it encourages and edifies those around you.

You may have no idea who in your circle is looking to you as an example of how to do singleness. Very possibly, someone in the wings is counting on you to fight it out.

THE TROUBLE WITH PORNOGRAPHY

As imperfect humans on this side of eternity, our sexual expression is subject to distortion and perversion, especially if we doubt God's goodness or aren't clear on why or how we ought to align our sexual desires with his direction. For me, a prolonged lack of clarity about God's purpose in my sexuality emerged as a struggle with pornography.

It didn't start off explicit. Like many others, my first exposure was inadvertent, when I was young and at a sleepover trying to fit in. Soon I snuck glimpses of soap operas and late-night sex help call-in shows, telling myself that I was simply interested in the drama and anatomy of it all. Over time, I allowed my eyes and ears to linger on Hollywood sex scenes, then maybe even rewind them or look for them online. Then I would search for more content.

I set some boundaries that I think protected me in some ways. For example, I never ventured outside YouTube. But every time I pulled up a video, it was a little act of rebellion towards God. And every time I rebelled, I felt a bit more distant from him.

My narrative went something like this: "God is withholding spouse and sex from me. Therefore, He owes me. I can't help it if I have to go elsewhere to get my needs met. At least I'm not sleeping around with a bunch of random guys, right?" It may seem obvious to you where I went wrong, but it has taken prayer, worship, confession to strategic people, counselling, and reflection to uncover the lies I digested and justification I concocted.

I had heard that porn was wrong, but it always seemed to be framed as a matter of avoiding it so as not to hurt one's spouse and sex life. The further away marriage and permissible sex seemed, the more I felt justified in keeping up the habit. So every time a pastor preached about staying away from porn to protect marriage, I mentally responded, "I'm probably not getting married, so what does it matter?"

What God is showing me faithfully and painfully over what seems to be far too long a time, is that spouse or not, sex or not, pornography damages my view of people, of God and of myself. With the thinking, entitlement, and judgmentalism involved, people become objects to meet my needs, God becomes a withholder who owes me something, and I become a reduction of my most animalistic tendencies. These same tenants underly the modern incel (involuntary celibate) movement that causes so much harm and has gained such infamy.

Anything that dehumanizes others is not from God and does not honour God. And nothing dehumanizes so quickly as using another person, or their image, for our own purposes, be they for pleasure, distraction, or a numbing agent. Pornography is all three. Whether it's pictures, videos, sex scenes, media from explicit websites, or even graphic descriptions in a romance novel, no version of pornography will keep the humanity of the subject intact. Every iteration sets up the consumer be both disappointed and disappointing in the context of reality.

To those who see engaging with pornography as natural, no big deal, or in the realm of an adult's choice, I will just share that, for me, as with most addictive patterns, it soon took on a life of its own.

Jesus explained this as the eyes being the lamp of the body: *"If your eyes are healthy, your whole body will be full of light. But if your eyes are unhealthy, your whole body will be full of darkness"* (Matthew 6:22–23). When I allow my eyes to take in darkness, my senses dim. Paul called it sowing to the flesh and reaping destruction (Galatians 6:8).

The problem with saying yes to sin in any way is that I don't have the ability to see how far my yes reaches. I may think I can handle the immediate consequences of a decision, but I never know what path that door will lead to. That path might lead to another yes I won't have the option to refuse. A yes today may mean giving up a future no. A yes today means telling myself I'm not worthy of a better life, and telling God that I don't trust him to give me one.

As an aside, these principles don't apply only to pornography. I've also had to consider other ways I entertain myself, and what it does to me emotionally. My brain definitely has a princess setting that I pop into when I watch a romantic movie or read a love story. While not inherently problematic, these stories can prey on me when I'm most vulnerable and keep me in a mental state that isn't helpful for either my singleness or my faith.

Many lies can surround a struggle with pornography and prevent a person from walking away. Out of disgust of a loathsome habit, it's easy to take an all-or-nothing stance and neglect to recognize incremental progress. In fearing exposure, we may try to deal with it on our own. While God is capable of miraculous healing, in my experience pornography and other addictive behaviours are rarely prayed away in a moment of secrecy. The very act of admitting that a struggle falls into a category of addiction can be healing. Not only do we have a promise of healing in the act of confession (James 5:16), we also have accountability. When we can admit the darkest truth to ourselves, it's because we're already stepping towards the light.

If you have struggled with pornography, you may think that struggle has caused you to think less of yourself, but it is more likely that a crisis of self-worth is what left you vulnerable to pornography. God wants to remind you of who you are. He wants to remind you of who he is. He wants to weave your story into something beautiful. He doesn't want to erase the parts of your story that embarrass you; he wants to redeem them and use them for the good of many. This is rarely accomplished in the silence of solitude.

If you're struggling with pornography, know that you're not alone and there is help. If you found the porn, you can find the help.

There is a bit less help available for women, but that is slowly changing. I would caution against believing that pornography, sex, and related issues are more difficult for men. However well-intentioned or gender-clarifying that sentiment is intended to be, it instantly limits conversation with a woman by minimizing her struggle. It can also reaffirm the lie to men that they can't control themselves. I'm not suggesting that it's the same for men and women, but we experience this issue differently enough that we need to stop comparing our challenges. We're just different. It isn't easy for anyone and the journey to recovery is a road less travelled for a reason.

EMBRACE YOUR BODY

Because of how often we neglect our bodies, I think we can become fixated on sexual release. We are so primed to value the intellectual over the physical experience, and so deprived of physical interaction, affection, and activity, that the only time some of us pay attention to our body is when we feel a sexual urge.

Read or watch the news with any regularity and you'll find a story that illuminates the tension between technological advancement and human interaction. We now have self-scanners and self-checkouts at grocery stores, not to mention the ability to do banking and shopping online. Various forms of artificial intelligence have replaced the need to interact with human service providers. Independent and often contactless delivery services can bring us nearly anything. These new realities have subtly and slowly removed slivers of truly human connection from our everyday lives.

As a rule, our modern Western paradigm is to be physically reserved and affection-avoidant. I'm reminded of this when I encounter other cultures who are much more physically and emotionally expressive.

On a visit to Eastern Europe, I was struck by the physical affection built into daily life through greetings that involve a kiss on either cheek. Similarly, I remember a Latina colleague of mine telling me, "You never need to ask me if I want a hug. I always want a hug." While it's okay to be reserved, and while technological advancements can be amazing, we would do well to recognize the impacts that physical isolation and distance can have on our bodies, including our hormones, nervous systems, and relationship to stimulation. We likely learned this more than ever during the social distancing and chaos that occurred during the pandemic of 2020.

I've come to realize how much the church can contribute to this physical affection deficit. Our theology often prioritizes mind, soul, and spirit wellness while neglecting the needs of the body. This encourages us to dissociate from our bodies and attribute to them the soulish moral struggles of what scripture calls "the flesh." The assumption is that our bodies are instruments that will betray us. In truth, "the flesh" is a way of depicting our fallen, sensual, and animalistic nature as humans[12] — or what we use our bodies for — and the source of sinful behaviour is frequently tied to the soul or metaphoric heart (Matthew 15:19, James 3:11–12).

The truth is that we are fearfully and wonderfully made (Psalm 139:14), were created in God's image (Genesis 1:27), can anticipate a resurrected body (1 Corinthians 15:35–58), and have a mandate to steward our bodies as temples of the Holy Spirit (1 Corinthians 6:19). My point is not to biblically justify vanity. It's to appreciate the function of the intricate layers of systems, organs, cells, and matter that make up our bodies.

Emerging research has found that both the gut and heart have intelligence and contain systems that function similar to brains. So when you say that you had a "gut feeling" about something, or that you knew something "in your heart," you may not be far from the truth.

Influenced by Eastern philosophies, the concept of listening to your body is becoming more prominent in North American wellness culture. Mindfulness and meditation movements urge us to be present. But these trends are still largely ignored and dismissed in many circles, including much of Christianity.

There's an old joke about academics that I think applies here:

> Q: Why do academics have bodies?
> A: To carry their brains to meetings.

The practices of the intellect can dull the voice of the body akin to hypnosis. Think of a time when you got so busy that you forgot to eat. Or when you were up late working on a project and suddenly realized it was 3:00 a.m. and you needed sleep. Or maybe you were so captured by a TV show or movie that you delayed a bathroom break until the point of panic.

I myself have been on a therapeutic journey that's alerted me to how much time I spend in my head and how little time I spend connected to and addressing my physical needs. My counsellor and I were working on me *being present*. I was very sceptical of this seemingly "hippie" advice but tried to do my homework in good faith.

One week, I left my appointment and did one of my favourite things to do professionally: I facilitated a half-day team retreat for a group of employees using a personality tool. I was absolutely in the zone—teaching, listening, facilitating activities, picking up on group dynamics, and making connections between individuals and the team's goals and values. I wasn't thinking about anything but what was going on in that room. My personal life and other work tasks were nicely stored in the back cupboard of my mind while I worked with the ingredients on the counter in front of me.

Afterwards I was so excited to tell my counsellor how present I had been. But as soon as I started to explain it to him, I realized that I had been caught not in a moment of presence, but in a moment of extreme inattention to my own needs. In fact, a wave of awareness had washed over me the moment the retreat concluded. That's when I realized how thirsty I was, how hungry I was, how desperately I needed a bathroom break, how sore my feet were from standing for four hours, and how fatigued I felt from exerting so much energy. I had ignored all these physical cues until they clamoured for my attention simultaneously.

No, I hadn't been present. I had been immersed and focused. Focus is important, and not inherently wrong, but for me this served as a real-life example of something I had gotten far too used to doing: ignoring the signals of my own body.

This inattention is what underlies many modern problems of over or under eating, exercising, sleeping, or medicating. Many modern medical dilemmas result from people learning to ignore the body's natural cues, and then mitigating the resulting problems by numbing themselves. When we ignore our bodies, they have a way of getting our attention. They may even hijack it. Think of the heart attack that serves as the wake-up call to an unhealthy lifestyle, or the panic attack that alerts you to your stress level. On a smaller scale, consider the cracked nailbeds that alert you to a lack of moisturizing and hydration.

If we're not careful we may only pay attention to our bodies when they're in crisis. This can affirm a false message pattern in our brains: anytime our body sends a signal we register, such as arousal, it must be an emergency.

The recent surge of research on burnout is a good reminder that the body needs attention now. If it doesn't get it, it will demand attention later. This is why we should take a proactive approach to cherishing the body and caring for it, as opposed to a reactive approach that attends to the body only when it has broken down.

This is about so much more than having a positive body image, although that too is important. Certainly we need to ensure that the messages we send and receive about the body are more than hateful glances in the mirror. We also need to ensure that the theology of our bodies is about more than mistrust and presumed betrayal.

When your body knows you can attend to it in pain and pleasure, it stops confusing the signals.

Even something as simple as shifting the narrative around personal grooming and health maintenance to a posture of self-love may help you pay attention to the messages you send yourself by brushing your teeth, working out, or trimming your nails. While we'll always need human connection, our own touch and activity can have healing properties too—rubbing our own feet, warming our own hands, scratching our own heads, exercising to the point of reaching an endorphin high, or even crossing and rubbing our arms in a self-hug.

Of course, we need to touch others, but being mindful of the body's requests for love and attention may reveal that this doesn't require a sexual component to be pleasurable, comforting, and fulfilling. This is the value of presence and attention or what may be called a human moment. Some have explored how a moment of connection with another limbic being has a soothing effect on the central nervous system.[13]

The question for the celibate single then isn't how you "get sex," but rather how can you take care of your body and introduce more physical and human connection in your life. Do you have family or friends with whom you can hold hands, hug, kiss, or maybe even cuddle? If not, can you start to introduce affection into existing or new relationships? When was the last time you went for a massage or pedicure or spa treatment or let a hairstylist play with your hair? How often do you opt for an in-person interaction rather than a digital or virtual one? Do you have pets you can pet and snuggle?

I grew up in a home that was largely anti-pharmaceutical. We were vaccinated, took antibiotics when we needed to, and had an assortment of painkillers, antacids, and ointments in our medicine cabinet.

But medicinal intervention was never the first step. If I had a headache as a teen, a pill was my parents' last suggestion after first addressing a long list of questions: "Have you eaten? Have you slept? Are you thirsty? Did you hit your head? Are your neck and shoulders tight? Are you upset? Have you been crying hard?" My parents assumed a multidimensional approach to pain relief before prescribing Tylenol. They assumed that a headache could be symptomatic of more than one thing and didn't jump straight to quick relief.

Sexual arousal can certainly be an issue, but it's not our only issue, and discovering and connecting with one's body can help to contextualize it. Arousal is a complex physical, mental, emotional, and spiritual experience that can be responded to in many ways apart from sexual release. Are you tired? Are you hungry? Are you sad? Are you lonely? What does your body need? I'm not trying to trivialize the power or value of libido, but it may be worth asking an important question when trying to manage sexual desire in the context of celibacy: "Do I need an orgasm or a hug?"

There are many nonsexual ways to achieve hormonal, physiological, and emotional responses that do our bodies and hearts a world of good. Sexual arousal isn't the enemy. But if it takes the lead in every story, it would be helpful to pay attention to our physicality.

In short, managing sexual desire, though never easy, is a simpler task when placed in the context of a balanced physical experience.

BE SEXY

I can be sexual without having sex! This was a liberating realization for me. I can do things that make me feel sexy: light candles, take long baths, listen to soft music, shop for pretty lingerie, buy beautiful clothes, and read or watch a romantic story, among other things. It can be a thrill to spend a bit more money on the matching undergarments to sit through a business meeting with the secret that I'm wearing the lacy red bra rather than the boring tan cotton one. I feel sexy while dancing around my apartment in a silky robe while I do my hair and makeup. My bed seems sexier when I spring for the high thread-count sheets and opt for some throw pillows. It feels good to go out to dinner in a dress I know I look amazing in, doing it just for me.

I'm not sure what makes you feel sexy to yourself, but I encourage you to figure it out. Is it the glisten of sweat on your muscles after a good workout that reminds you to appreciate your own body? Is it a piercing or tattoo that reminds you, even under the armour of everyday life, that you have a sensual side? Is there an outfit in which you feel like a million bucks? Is there a brand of cologne or perfume that makes you feel just a little more attractive?

There may be different lines for you to colour within. Maybe some of my suggestions seem silly, or others too easily carry you to a lustful place. And I'm still working out how all this celibacy stuff applies to masturbation, another topic I think we over-vilify and under-understand. I've engaged with interesting Christian interpretations that are both for and against masturbation, and I think they're all a little right. I do think it can be difficult to spend time in that activity and not shift into lust, fantasy, covetousness, pornography, or addiction... but I wouldn't say that it's impossible, nor would I want to perpetuate the damaging myth that pleasure is the same thing as sin.

This is another reason why it's so important to manage our sexuality from our relationship with God, and why that relationship should be informed by scripture instead of being static or stuck. It's also a reason to have vulnerable relationships in which we can think through and discuss these subjects in the context of friendship, rather than defaulting to secrecy and shame.

DO NOT BE ASHAMED

When it comes to stewarding sexual desire, there are many approaches. Regardless of how we manage it, I think it's important to release ourselves from shame and be curious about how closely we link sexuality and identity. Desire is God-given and sanctification is a process. As God provides revelation in an area, we can work to bring it under submission. But we must also have compassion and acceptance for the parts of ourselves that will always be imperfect, and the parts of the journey that will always be a struggle.

The mercy of the cross is that the work of reconciliation is already done. We don't need to have our sex stuff all sorted out before we approach God for insight and empowerment. We can approach him knowing that he accepts us as we are and that we have already been redeemed. We can greet our sexual selves from the position of spiritual victory.

Celebrating and seeking to understand my sexuality seems like a much better option than hating myself into a different version of myself or wishing for another life.

THE DESIRES OF YOUR HEART

*If we find ourselves with a desire that nothing in this
world can satisfy, the most probable explanation is
that we were made for another world.*[14]
—C.S. Lewis

A RECURRING STAR among the prayers that fall into the take-pain-away category is the request for God to remove my desire for marriage. It just seems to me like the single life would be easier without it.

Interestingly, I have lots of desires that don't cause me pain and which I don't even think about praying away or consider being mad at God about. For example, I'd love to fly first-class someday, but that doesn't prevent me from travelling on a budget. I can't think of a time where, in passing the spaciousness of first class, I asked God to remove my jealousy in order to make economy seating feel more luxurious.

But when it comes to my desire for marriage, I have often felt deprived. I've grumbled at God for putting me in this position. I don't like desiring, wanting, or hoping in this area. I strongly feel the heartsickness of deferred hope (Proverbs 13:12).

I think we sometimes seek fulfilled desire for the sake of closure and control. We aren't very good at holding space for longing. Either we rush to fulfill it or actively try to kill it. Sometimes we even find death more comfortable than life. We'd rather let a dream die, an idea fade, a plan tarnish and crust over, than hold out for a hope that is yet to be fulfilled. It's often easier to grow accustomed to mourning than to steward the faith of anticipation. We may call this maturity, realism, or pragmatism when in actuality it's cynicism.

But what if some desires are meant to be experienced rather than attained? Our human perspective of desire is often about driving to the finish line, but what if fulfilment is more a continuous process than a static, stable end, more a water fountain or overflowing cup (Psalm 23:5) than a completed checklist? While we're busy pursuing happy endings, God is inviting us into a life that will never end. While we want a destination to fulfill us, he offers an inspiring journey. There is a fluid nature to desire and fulfillment, and entering the abundant and eternal life God promises will at some point require us to get acquainted with the concept of longing.

As the psalmist commends us, *"delight yourself in the Lord; And He will give you the desires of your heart"* (Psalm 37:4, NASB). Aligning with God both shapes what we want and fulfills what we want. When we fix our eyes on Jesus, he both plants seeds of desire and harvests the fruit of desire in us.

But we are in error when we assume that this is a cause-and-effect relationship. We set ourselves up for disappointment when we presume that all desire can, will, and should be fulfilled this side of heaven. We mock the throne of grace when we delight in God only for what he can do for us.

Experiencing the desire for marriage may not mean I am fulfilled by marriage, but aligning myself with God means that I don't have to resent the desire for marriage, as it is a holy thing, and I can expect to be fulfilled even if I never marry. God has ways of digging deeper anyway. Is it marriage I seek, or is it a deeper longing for relationship and intimacy? Is it children I want, or to love and be loved and influence the next generation? Am I actually delighting in the Lord, or am I trying to leverage my faith as a means of getting something I want?

Sometimes we create desires ourselves. This can be extra confusing for Christians because we have a hard time distinguishing between the spiritual and the hormonal. It's made more difficult if we mistakenly assume that, by following God, any whim we have is Holy-Spirit-directed. This is worsened still when we affirm that myth by praying about something over and over again, causing the desire to grow stronger.

So how can we discern the Holy Spirit's planting of a seed from our own obsessive thinking? How do we know when we're experiencing a holy want versus being ruled by our own urges? How can we manage rather than resolve the tension caused by desire?

It's almost as if there is a spot in the human brain where the last person you were romantically interested in resides. And it doesn't seem to matter whether the feelings are still active or not, whether a real or imagined connection ended willingly, or whether it has been days, weeks, months, or even years since the last encounter. Whenever romantic thoughts are triggered, the mind wanders back, and that same face bursts into memory. This continues until the object of affection is replaced by a new interest.

If this is true, it's one reason why the stereotype of the rebound relationship has so much power. Rebounding is a quick way to interrupt the cycle by at least temporarily dethroning the last king or queen of your heart.

Many singles have told me that such feelings are a sign that they'll find a romantic relationship someday. They believe that unless the desire is totally dead in them, it must mean they are meant to be in a relationship. Often they use very strong spiritual or fatalistic language; they "just know" or feel God has "promised" it, or perhaps they "sense in their spirit" that they wouldn't have to wrestle with such feelings if they were meant to be single.

I've so been there. When my heart is gripped so strongly, I can feel powerless. But the reality is that the strength is usually of my own making.

Several years ago, I remember getting really hung up on a guy I met online. We messaged back and forth for several weeks before meeting in person. By the time I actually got my eyes and ears on him, I was already seventy-five percent ready to start a relationship, even though I hadn't had a chance to assess anything other than our written communication.

Tragically and thankfully, he didn't feel the same way and sent me a Dear Jane communication that same evening. While this now reads as ridiculous as a sitcom script, even to me, it actually took me quite a bit of time to get over that rejection. I met the man only once, but I invested big time. My thoughts, prayers, messages, and borderline-stalker internet "research" had all positioned this guy in the centre of my focus for weeks. Even when I wasn't actively engaged in communicating with him, I had been selecting words for how I would describe my current activity the next time I wrote. I had been determining how to suss out his political views without seeming nosey or controlling. I jumped out of my skin at every message notification I received all day and planned what I would wear to our first encounter.

Had a romantic relationship resulted, people would have called that the puppy love stage, or the honeymoon period. But in reality, it was about my heart getting caught up in the exact direction my mind tried to take it. This same psychology explains the success of lotteries and casinos, which appeal to people who buy into the idea of a dream so much that they start planning their lives around the outcome.

Infatuation is where addiction science and relationship science overlap. The brain likes the simplicity of repetitive patterns and will always find the quickest and easiest route to pleasure. Scripture describes this pattern in terms of investment: *"For where your treasure is, there your heart will be also"* (Matthew 6:21). Wherever we place value, that will dictate the direction in which our hearts move. The heart automatically follows our deposits of money, time, thought, emotion, and even prayer. This powerful principle can be used for great good. Jesus even instructs his followers to pray for our persecutors and enemies (Matthew 5:44) because he knows our hearts will move towards them when we do so. Through our prayers, God grants us the ability to make things happen in, what Darrell Johnson calls, "the dignity of causality."[15]

When you've spent hours thinking about, praying for, and fantasizing about someone or something, you've sold that person or thing part of your heart. But if and when you're done with that person or thing, you sort of have to buy your heart back.

The good news is that our hearts will eventually catch up and move on, at least partially, when we shift our investment. But the same way investment happens over time, so does reinvestment. You have to direct that energy somewhere else. It takes time and intention and can be complicated by other investments that aren't retrievable. We do this constructively by deepening other relationships, developing a strength, leveraging a talent, finding ways to serve, and expanding our spiritual lives. Or we do this destructively by attaching to activities, habits, and people that don't add to us, yet hungrily sap us of resources that were once committed elsewhere.

People often share with me that they've asked God to take away their desire for marriage, or their feelings for another person. And when he doesn't do it, they stall out. They may even believe that this stalling is a sign that they aren't gifted enough at singleness or that God must have a plan to make the romance work, even if there is much evidence to the contrary.

But the trick to managing our desires has nothing to do with God removing the desire; it's about us no longer investing in them. To do this requires us to focus more on the nature of who God is, and our need of and love for him, than on what we're asking him to do for us.

I'm not saying that your particular desire is wrong, or even that it isn't God-given, but I believe it can exist latently without being fed every day. What remains of a specific desire after we starve it of attention is the substance worth talking about. After all, our focus of delight is supposed to be the desire-giver, not the desire itself. The stuff on top, the obsession, is solved by taking captive our thought lives (2 Corinthians 10:5). Our brains and hearts need a new king!

Of course, you'll want to be married more strongly if you constantly think about it, read about it, view life through a marriage lens, and dare I say even constantly pray about it. There are books, preachers, and social media influencers who instruct singles to do all of the above.

While I believe a single can hold a desire for marriage in a healthy way, I don't believe constant investment in the idea of romance is the answer to living a fulfilled life. This is why I often counsel my fellow singles to actually stop praying about their relationship status for a while, or to try entrusting those requests to a friend or family member who can pray over the details on their behalf. That way, they are free to focus on the here and now.

That's also why it's so important to pray about more than just one thing. Limiting our prayers to one topic narrows our perspective on God's will. It also limits our awareness to what he's doing in our lives and the lives of those around us.

When my prayers become a broken record, I fixate on God saying no to me. This persuades me to believe he doesn't answer prayer at all, since I'm missing the many yeses that may be waiting for me—if I would only ask. We need to pray about more than our singleness to expand our conversation with God, bolster our faith, and remind ourselves how much bigger life is than this one topic that has us in its grip.

In J.K. Rowling's *Harry Potter and the Philosopher's Stone*, the Mirror of Erised serves as an object lesson about this kind of fixation. The magical mirror alters itself to match the deepest dreams of whomever looks into it. While initially heartwarming, the mirror soon becomes so tantalizing to the onlooker that they forget about pursuing reality. This is why the sage Dumbledore warns Harry, "It does not do to dwell on dreams and forget to live, remember that."[16]

If you want a desire to really shift, you need to stop fixating on that which mirrors your dreams back at you all the time. This requires moving your attention, prayers, time, money, conversation, reading material, and entertainment to something else. This is how you can be powerfully *"transformed by the renewing of your mind"* (Romans 12:2).

It's not enough to just stop investing in one portfolio. The key is to transfer your investments to others. In the case of desiring marriage, reinvesting in embracing singleness can be a great start.

The lie single people easily digest is that marriage is an answer, while assuming there are no other questions. This myth is easily debunked by the many married people who now sit across from their spouses and secretly wonder why they still want something more. Whether married or single, all humans wrestle with the concept of longing. We all have a thing that is yet to be satisfied within us; when we stop calling that thing a romantic relationship, we are faced with the unsettling and wondrous depths of a God we can't fully understand.

The ability to desire is mysterious, beautiful, sacred, and holy, yet it is not to be feared. There are visceral, continual, and intentional qualities to desire that are meant to help us glimpse eternity. Our longing whispers to us of something unseen, something yet to be. Desire is the foreshadowing of heaven, the divine lever, the ultimate hoping in what we do not have (Romans 8:25), and the pulley[17] that draws us to the Father. Desire is the call to worship.

We were designed to worship. It's the default human position. To exalt, glorify, and revere is a state we come by easily. We don't often call it worship, but we participate in it regularly by attributing worth to what we value through fandom, celebrity culture, sport, the arts, entertainment, salesmanship, politics, employment hierarchies, brand allegiance, and social media. We are fans, devotees, groupies, roadies, followers... in other words, worshippers. David Foster Wallace went so far as to say, "There is no such thing as not worshipping."[18]

In his love, God invites us into his triune relationship to worship him—Father, Son, and Spirit—knowing how much that will satisfy us. God does not demand our worship out of need or narcissism; he invites us into the complete worship the Trinity already has going on, knowing that our deepest desire can be truly satisfied in only one way. This desire gives us a glimpse of the eternity God has set in our hearts (Ecclesiastes 3:11). Our longing points us to him, our talents and skills becoming ways to express praise. And if we are wise, like King Solomon, we will respond not by seeking the fruit of desire but rather the discerning heart that can withstand its weight (1 Kings 3:1–14).

But this longing can feel like a curse rather than a gift when we attempt to satisfy it with something that isn't God. These gifts fill with the weight of burden when we try to shoulder them by our own strength. When we step out of position and forget that it is God who is to fulfill his plans, we are prone to fear both that our dreams won't come true and that they will, both that our talents won't be effective and that they will. Out of position, we are prone to dread hope and tremble at the unknown, and in so doing, we misdirect our worship towards things that limit the world to a size we can manage. Soon we fulfill our hunger and thirst for eternity with behaviours and habits and people that numb pain and possibility.

Our futures become limited, since the distractions we conjure are brief. My friend Mark Buchanan put it to me this way: "All the fulfillments and satisfactions this side of heaven are about thirty minutes long. Then the ache comes back." And it comes back because none of these non-God people, things, or habits were built to withstand the power and pressure of our undying attention.

Nevertheless, the cycle of trying and failing to achieve our hearts' desire becomes familiar, and familiarity becomes comfortable, and soon comfort itself becomes the object of worship.

Bruce Marshall once said that "the young man who rings the bell at the brothel is unconsciously looking for God."[19] When we pursue our longings in our own way, we sometimes wonder where God is, but the truth is that he is right at the centre of what we long for. The desire for sex, marriage, children, and the linear familial path, though all good things, aren't the real desire. Nor is the desire for freedom, independence, and autonomy. Recognizing this doesn't mean we all have to become nuns and priests and marry Jesus, though perhaps my Catholic friends are on to something. However, it can cause us to pause and consider whether God is still answering our first prayer, which was probably some version of, "God, help!" Perhaps we have learned to sing the songs of surrender, but we need to rehearse the worship of a truly surrendered life. When I'm pursuing my dream, I have to do it in my strength, which inevitably runs out. But when I pursue God's dream for me, I gain access to his strength which never ends.

God knows us better than we know ourselves. He knows the answer to the prayer we didn't realize we were praying all along. When he asks what we want, we sometimes answer out of our own smallness rather than acknowledging his greatness. Our freedom lies in the paradigm shift.

Two of Jesus's disciples, James and John, were with him when he asked, *"What do you want me to do for you?"* (Mark 10:36) They got *the* question and, in their smallness, they postured for political position and asked to be important, to sit at his right hand.

But only a few verses later, after being asked the same question, blind, begging Bartimaeus answered: *"Rabbi, I want to see"* (Mark 10:51).

Maybe you desire sex. Maybe you desire marriage. Maybe you'll get them. Maybe you won't. But what do you really want? What are you afraid to want? What might God have for you beyond the simple question and answer loop you've been stuck in? Are you committed to your love goggles or do you want to really see?

Desire

"What do you want?" I hear the Spirit ask me.
"To be a bride," my pattern answers.
"What do you really want?" He knows better.
"To be your bride," I learn to say.
"What do you want me to do for you?" A Saviour's gentle provocation.
I seek the courage to admit it. "Show me your way."

OPEN TO LOVE

We accept the love we think we deserve.[20]
—Stephen Chbosky

IN MY TWENTIES, I lived in a region notorious for an extremely high man-to-woman ratio in the population. It was common among the few women who lived there to joke about the ample romantic opportunities.

At one point, a single friend of mine was asked how she hadn't been able to find someone when the odds were so in her favour. Her response? "The odds may be good, but the goods are a little odd!"

Jokes aside, most people assume there is more to a romantic partnership than mere availability. But if the goal of adulthood is to end up in a couple, then singles are constantly failing. And when it feels like that, it's easy to question our approach to dating, romance, and partner selection. We may even be told we're "too picky" or "not open enough." Sometimes, in our zeal to find a partner, or maybe in reaction to external pressures, we throw out the concept of partner suitability altogether.

In this territory, we find the dating horror stories or unhappy tales of those who end up with partners who don't share their faith or values at a core level, stereotypically fall for the bad guy or bad girl routine, or otherwise end up in low compatibility relationships. Some couples find themselves trapped in cycles of violence, online fraud, or manipulation.

What's worse is that we can get really spiritually confused about all this. We may ask, "If I believe in a God of grace, mercy, forgiveness, and love, who am I to rule out a romantic partner for any of the above reasons? How can I say they aren't good enough for me when they're good enough for God?" I don't think the answers are easy, but they are simple.

I once heard a speaker say that we have to debunk our own notion of soulmates and get back to the concept that God made everyone, that we just need to pick a person and follow Christ's example for how to love them. I like this idea in principle. Love is most certainly a choice. Arranged marriages attest to this idea, and divorce can often be retraced to the fallacy of the importance of falling for the "right person."

We can too easily trust more in the idea of a perfect partner than in the reality of a perfect God. This puts pressure on us to find someone to complete us in ways only God can fulfill, giving us an excuse to abdicate our responsibility about loving and living well regardless of how imperfect our relationships end up being. It also reduces God's plans for us to a singular will-he-won't-he narrative.

But romantic love isn't unconditional by default, and that's problematic when it's that love which takes the lead in generating couple relationships. Romantic love motivates us to customize, maybe even falsify, our online profiles and dating personas to secure a match. Romantic love fuels our post-modernity and makes us look for the experience of love before the decision of love. So when we say things like "Love conquers all," are we talking about the God-empowered, grace-infused love that never fails? Or is it the human-established, hormone-infused fog that eventually lifts?

How to love is certainly key to any discussion about relational longevity. But when it comes to romantic partnership, the question of *who* we commit to is important. This is especially true in an individualistic society in which we often work in opposition to the factors that empower long-term commitment—namely, selflessness. While it may be futile to discuss relationships in moralizing terms of right or wrong, it's helpful to consider whether a pairing is wise or compatible. This concept of relational equity is fairly common even outside Christianity. Of course, there are always outliers where a seemingly doomed romance beats the odds, but even in these cases there are usually some core unifying factors or values.

Why does this all matter in the context of a single seeking romance? Because when a single person's life gets difficult, desperation can cause us to make dumb dating decisions.

To clarify, I don't believe there's any such thing as a perfect person when it comes to romance. In fact, I think the notion of soulmates and courtship culture have put far too much pressure on Christians in the dating process. By kissing dating goodbye,[21] the church forgot that relationships involve a journey of exploration, imitation, mutual influence, and growth. Healthy dating may very well be part of self-discovery, not just a spousal vetting process.

As a side note to friends of singles, healthy dating is much easier in the context of a community that doesn't tease us incessantly about our flirtations like we're still in high school. If a romance is legitimate, you're insulting something close to our hearts; if it isn't, you're making it more awkward than it already is.

Being single, desiring marriage, and pursuing romance involves risk, curiosity, and uncertainty as we navigate partnerships and pairings. While we may act with an eye towards marriage, the process is no less spiritual just because it doesn't result in a union. In fact, I think we need to question the entire concept of so-called "failed relationships." Is it failing to have tried something? Is it failing to have acknowledged it wasn't working and ended it? Is it failing to have learned and grown in the process? Why is any relationship that hasn't achieved permanence considered a failure?

I think it's hubris to assume we must meet all the criteria for marriage before going on a first date, and arrogance to think we could determine that such criteria are met without actually dating. However, while it's cynical to think nobody in the world could be a suitable romantic partner, it's folly to overlook how a person's character and behaviour impact their capacity for relational longevity. And it's presumptuous to assume that God's grace will make up for our own lack of wisdom.

I have struggled to make peace with the fact that it's okay to have standards, preferences, and wants in seeking a partner. When I've felt ambivalent about my singleness, these ideas have felt like judgments that preclude me from having a romantic life. But finding confidence in singleness empowers me to respect myself and not apologize for how I want to behave and be treated.

To seek someone who's open and aligned with you about important topics such as faith, theology, money, sex, mental health, addiction, physical health, previous partners, children from prior relationships, future childrearing, politics, morality, family, friends, interests, careers, and goals is not judgmental. It's okay to want a partner to add to your life and make you better. It's okay to be picky and have deal-breakers. And in seeking romance, it's okay to forgo a relationship unless or until a person steps into your life with a combination of these qualities. This isn't about promoting the myth of a perfect partner, exacerbating the legalism of a perfect self, or condemning yourself or others for past behaviour; it's about admitting that lasting relationships require a strong foundation and that the formation of this foundation can be disrupted. It's also about creating a life that is so worth living that we exercise caution in introducing a partner to it. In my search for somebody, nobody is better than just anybody.

I'm sure this type of discernment has been used as an excuse for prejudice. There's a fine line between being mindful of the company we keep and adopting moral superiority. Of course, all these wants, hopes, and plans must be surrendered to God. And while he may expose your own brokenness, redeem your own failings, sand down the edges of your own perfectionism, and provide you with grace to accept a whole range of choices in yourself and others, that doesn't mean you're legalistic, judgmental, or unforgiving for valuing the evidence of character or the wisdom of compatibility in a potential partner.

The scriptures support discernment in selecting leaders (Titus 1:6–9), determining companionship (Proverbs 13:20), assigning offices of the church (1 Timothy 3:1–7), and in articulating the qualities of a desirable spouse (Deuteronomy 24:5, Proverbs 31:10, Ruth 2–4), and we are free to do the same. At the end of the day, a good tree will produce good fruit (Matthew 7:17–20) and a healthy relationship will produce and draw out life, light, and expansiveness in you.

I believe dating can be a healthy part of managing Christian singleness, but the process of discernment is difficult in isolation. The physical, chemical, biological, emotional, and spiritual powers of romantic love, physical attraction, and sexual desire are immense, destabilizing, and nearly impossible to navigate with a completely clear head, and even more challenging if we're motivated by anxiety or desperation. This is one reason why community is so important for singles. We need clear-sighted, scripturally grounded, Holy Spirit-guided, experience-infused counsel to help us navigate the path of grace.

The late Jane Austen often visited this idea of romantic selection. In her classic novel *Pride and Prejudice*, the heroin Elizabeth Bennet rejects a proposal from the dim-witted Mr. Collins, forfeiting the guaranteed security of coupledom for the hope of a more fulfilling life. Conversely, her friend Charlotte Lucas, a near-spinster at 27, accepts Mr. Collins over a life of singleness. (Did anyone else have a panic attack when they realized they were older than her?) As readers, we hope for and later realize Elizabeth pairing up with a far more agreeable choice in Mr. Darcy (who is also pretty obtuse at first). However, as the story unfolds it is clear that our Lizzy didn't know the future when she rejected first Mr. Collins and then Mr. Darcy (at first). In those moments, she wasn't choosing one man over another, she was choosing self-respect over a life of mediocrity.[22]

Obviously, this is fiction and satire. But it's still poignant when you consider that Austen wrote in an era when single women couldn't choose a life of non-partnership without fearing a lack of career, finance, property, or voice. It's also helpful to recall that Austen herself remained unmarried.

For many singles, it would be too risky to make a decision similar to Elizabeth's. They would rather make a coupled life work than move forward without the guarantee. Others would rather be spinsters than be with a Mr. Collins, regardless of whether a Mr. Darcy exists.

We're all wired a little differently. We're attracted to, and have grace for, different qualities. I'm not saying we should all be the same, but it's okay to hope for certain characteristics even if you never get them. There are worse things in life than being unmarried.

When I say something like, "It's okay to want a partner you find attractive," nobody ever disagrees with me. Yet when I say, "It's okay to want a partner who doesn't struggle with addiction," people push back. "But what about grace?" they ask.

In his letter to the people of Corinth, the apostle Paul wrote that everything is permissible, but not everything is beneficial (1 Corinthians 10:23). For so long, we have divided the dating pool into right and wrong, saint and sinner, soulmate and non-soulmate. We have neglected a simpler truth—that dating, romance, and marriage may not always be beneficial, either for us or for others.

This is a hard truth to digest in a culture that idolizes romantic love. You don't need to look further than the entertainment industry to know that many see romance as a reward. People literally compete for it in some reality TV contexts! They see romance almost as a human right. Nearly every movie has at least one plotline that doesn't resolve satisfactorily until a character finds their romantic pairing. When we think of romance as a kind of prize—or worse, that singleness is some kind of punishment—we feel ungracious when we withhold romance. We hold to Jesus's ideals enough to tout that everyone is deserving of love, but forget that his love isn't limited to romantic expression.

Everyone is worthy of love, but love and romance aren't the same thing. Just because a person is *saveable* doesn't mean they are maritally *suitable*. Forgivable isn't the same as relationally compatible. Redemption doesn't negate a disparity of experience. Somewhere amongst the extremes of making rigid checklists to interview prospective spousal candidates, becoming embittered at a lack of suitable options, and flinging wide the doors to any person with a pulse is the process of discernment. This doesn't make marriage more exclusive or Godlike; it actually shows that marriage is limited in its ability to express the love of the Father for us all.

I'm not saying that marriage is a higher calling. I'm actually arguing that it's tangential to the ultimate future that God has for us. We may have erred in forgetting that our future is life with the Father, not life with a spouse. I'm not suggesting that we sort people into categories of worthy and unworthy. My point is that when we stop equating marriage with salvation, we broaden our ability to relate to the many people God has brought into our lives. When we think beyond romantic love, we truly begin to implement the concept of loving our neighbours unconditionally.

Yes, God made all men and women. He calls us believers and children. He shows us how to love each other. But let's not mistake the love of God or the love of our brothers and sisters in Christ for human romance. While marriage is a gift, it's not the ultimate gift God can give us. He already gave that gift: his son, Jesus Christ.

God can redeem anything, but that's because he's God. In his relationship with us, he does the heavy lifting and makes up for our lack. When we seek this type of dynamic in our romance, we play the role of rescuer thinking that somehow we are more gracious or forgiving than God. We may even conclude that our love will be what finally fixes someone. Only our saviour Jesus can tread this path.

It's true that we must love our neighbours as we love ourselves. But if I don't love myself very much, I can only offer a distorted counterfeit of love to others. When I fully embrace God's forgiveness of my own sins, I don't need to hide behind the brokenness of others. When I internalize the message of the cross, I need not compensate for another's failings. When I understand the truth of forgiveness, I can see that exercising romantic discernment isn't the same thing as withholding love. When I know that I'll always have the love of God, I need not frantically settle for a romantic relationship to fill me up.

The most loving thing you might be able to do for someone is to acknowledge that a romantic entanglement now may be the worst thing for their future, healing, and spiritual walk. The most loving thing you might be able to do for yourself is to recognize that a romantic partnership may throw you off-mission.

You are never beyond redemption. In Christ, you are always enough. But that doesn't mean every romantic relationship contains the ingredients for long-term health or mutual edification. When we break free of the assumption that marriage is the ultimate expression of love, we find relief in not having to find a romantic match for everyone we meet. When we broaden the definition of fulfillment beyond coupledom, we realize that God has new beginnings in mind for us all. He is too good a storyteller, too great a lover, to let every plot resolve in human romance.

It may seem as though I err on the side of staying single over entering a relationship. I suppose that's a little bit true. I still love marriage. I even desire it. There is beauty in the idea of two imperfect people sacrificing their personal preferences to join together as one.

But somewhere along the way we got the love story wrong. The wedding that's open to everyone is the one between Christ and the church. It's Easter, not Valentine's Day, that signals the greatest love story ever told — the one in which God is reconciled with his people, sacrificing himself out of love for all so that life, light, and wholeness defeat death, darkness, and disconnection.

You are included in this grand romance by a God who is madly in love with you. You need not settle for anything less.

Nine

MY CHOICE

*You have brains in your head. You have feet in
your shoes. You can steer yourself
any direction you choose.*[23]
—Dr. Seuss

MY FRIEND AND I once brunched at a hipster eatery in the suburbs complete with industrial lighting, wood pallet panelling, and pretentious menu flourishes like lavender lattes and cashew butter. Having done all but one of our more than fifteen years of friendship in different cities since bonding in our freshman year, we averaged one face-to-face meetup every three to four years. A long triannual meal was our chance to reminisce and catch up on life—family, church, school, work, health, romance, and milestones. We talked about our successes, failures, and broken hearts. Whether describing joy or sadness, I hung on her every word as encouragement that I wasn't alone in being single while also trying to follow Jesus.

Suddenly she said something surprising: "My counsellor told me that if I wanted to be in a relationship, I would be. And I realized… that's actually true."

I let my default reaction of resistance pass through me in order to take in the words with a fresh perspective.

"Me too," I replied, the words slowly tumbling off my lips as I both realized and confessed them at the same time.

Singleness is a choice. As soon as someone states this outright, I immediately jump to all the "yeah buts" and "what abouts" that seem to disprove the assertion. For example, I'll remember those who have lost a partner to death, been abandoned, or tried every type of dating app or setup opportunity they can find. I get frustrated when my quest for a meaningful relationship is reduced to something akin to an Amazon cart, as if relationships come made to order. If it's as easy as choosing to find someone, and I haven't, does that make me a failure?

Still, I think there is merit and freedom to the idea that we have a lot more control and influence over our relationship statuses than we may want to admit.

The result of not getting what we want can perpetuate the myth that we didn't choose where we are. And if you're like me, it's much easier to think that singleness is something that happened to you, not something you chose. I don't often feel like I'm choosing to be single. Rather, I feel like it has been thrust upon me. In such a state, it seems that to own my singleness as a choice is a failure.

Yet I know that a key to cultivating agency and avoiding victimhood is to take ownership of the aspects of my life that are in my sphere of control. And I've slowly and begrudgingly recognized that my singleness is more within that sphere than I want to concede.

Acceptance commitment therapy (ACT) is a therapeutic school of thought originated by Dr. Steven C. Hayes which explores pain and discomfort from the assumption that we often make our own suffering unnecessarily worse.[24]

The idea is that there are two categories of pain: clean discomfort and dirty discomfort.

Clean discomfort is the type of pain that just happens beyond your control. This might involve random events you can't predict or influence, such as loss, injury, or death. These usually involve their own emotional responses and grief process.

Dirty discomfort is the layer of suffering we add on top of clean discomfort through self-criticism, worry, control, complaining, avoiding, and resisting. It involves thoughts such as "I'm stupid," "I should be over this by now," "I'll never get it done," and "I'm sure I can fix this if I try hard enough!"

A common metaphor to explain this is quicksand. Though quicksand likely isn't the real-world threat many of us anticipated when we were children, entertainment has informed us that the best chance of surviving a fall into quicksand is to hold still until help comes. Thrashing about and struggling causes you to sink faster.

The point of the metaphor is to work on trying to process and move through clean discomfort without adding unnecessary suffering and resistance.

When we view singleness as something that's imposed on us, we often make the experience worse than it needs to be. We reject it, avoid it, and blame others, as well as God, for inflicting it upon us. The experience is less joyful and more miserable.

While the clean discomfort of grief, abandonment, and disappointment may contribute to your current state of singleness, there is likely at least part of your relationship status that is a result of the choices you've made.

So while I may not have looked into my future from the past and aimed my path at singleness, upon looking back I can see how the choices I've made have in part led me here.

For some, the choice to be single is easy. You may have even skimmed the last few paragraphs and asked, "What's the big deal?" Perhaps you don't desire a relationship and are truly satisfied with your oneness. Maybe contentment comes easily for you, or perhaps you don't have to work at enjoying being on your own.

For a long time, I was mystified by such people, and I still sometimes wrestle with the idea of choice. It can be difficult to think of enjoying singleness and wanting marriage as mindsets that aren't mutually exclusive. Because marriage is something I want, resistance rises up in me when someone implies that I have chosen against it. But the reality is that I have prioritized value, meaning, purpose, being spirit-led, and many other things above just finding a partner. That doesn't mean those who have found partners don't prioritize these things too, but in my case these priorities have limited my romantic options. While I may not have wished for the outcome of singleness, I have led my life in such a way that brought me to where I am today.

It's possible that those same choices may lead to marriage somewhere down the road.

In reality, I see that I could have played my cards differently to be with someone—if that had been my primary goal. I could have chosen an education that would have increased my odds of finding a husband, such as if I had attended Bible college. I could have continued to live in a city with a higher ratio of eligible men. I could have joined the party scene and engaged in hookup culture. I could have chosen a career field less intimidating to the opposite sex. I could have reciprocated flirtations and advances with men who held different values than me. I could have made changes to my physical appearance to make me more attractive in particular contexts. I could have spent much more time dating online.

In all these situations, the path I took seemed obvious to me. But that doesn't mean each wasn't a choice. I could view every decision I've made up until now as choosing *against* marriage, but in most cases, I was merely choosing *for* something else.

This is similar to my travel bucket list. When someone asks me what destination I most want to travel to, I always answer, "Greece." Yet at the time of writing this, with several vacations and travel expenditures under my belt, I still haven't been there. It's not that I don't want to go, and it's not that I think I will never go, but my life has unfolded in such a way as to prioritize other pursuits, whether they be related to work, family, or budget. This has all filtered through my decision-making process in a way that keeps me from prioritizing Greece.

So I can both say that I truly desire to go to Greece and that I have so far chosen not to go there. I wasn't deciding *against* going to Greece; I was deciding *for* other priorities, such as taking a work trip to the East Coast and tagging some vacation time while there.

I both want to be married and, so far, have chosen singleness. That doesn't mean I never pursue romance. Not every choice I've made has been against romance but rather in favour of a multitude of other activities, relationships, and opportunities.

You may be fighting with this internally, saying to yourself, "I don't have a choice since there's no one to date where I live" or "I didn't choose to have a sick family member to take care of" or "I didn't choose to work three jobs and have no social life." I would respectfully and compassionately disagree. Those are not easy choices, but they are choices all the same. You are choosing a city, church, career, and community despite the romantic ramifications. You are deciding that not just anyone can engage with you in your world. Paying your rent and eating meals are justifiably more important than making time for a social life. It's respectable for family matters to take precedence over dating. Maybe compatibility is more important to you than companionship.

While you may not have chosen all your circumstances, you do choose your responses. And if you're single, it means that certain things matter to you more than romance, whether it's spirituality, family, community, career, longevity, commitment, proximity to your hobbies, or the ability to travel. These things may matter to you more than you consciously know.

I actually think this is a good thing! There are many people who have prioritized romance and companionship over everything else to their own regret.

Please don't misunderstand me. I'm so happy for my friends and family members who have made choices to be in romantic partnerships. I think romantic love is beautiful and wonderful. I think lifelong commitment is noble and difficult. My own heart flutters at the prospect of maybe one day being one of those people. But I'm also happy when I see a single thriving in their mission, rejoicing in their freedom, and worshipping their Saviour. I don't think singleness is necessarily a better, harder, or worthier path, or even that the path is always permanent, but I do believe it is a chosen path.

I'm sure there are people who use their singleness as a barrier to intimacy and community, whose freedom borders on selfishness, or whose relationship status is a convenient way of avoiding accountability and risk, but I think such occurrences are rarer than we would like to admit. I believe there are many who aren't single for a lack of options, or a lack of interest, but for a lack of seeing coupledom as the ultimate pursuit. They respect themselves and the lives they lead too much to settle for guaranteed okayness over the possibility of greatness.

Singleness may not be entirely your choice, and it may not be your forever choice, but taking responsibility for what *is* allows you the agency and courage to step into a life of purpose, fulfilment, and freedom.

Do I want to be married someday?

Yes.
Am I choosing to be single?
Yes! Yes, I am!

GOD'S CHOICE

Who said anything about safe? Course he isn't safe. But he's good. He's the King, I tell you.[25]
—C.S. Lewis

CONSIDERING THE ROLE of our choice in singleness raises the question of the role of God's choice in our singleness. How we understand the sovereignty of God can greatly impact how we experience our relationship status.

There is prudence in being intentional about our days on the earth. After all, we are active players in our lives, not passive audience members. But as thoroughly, prayerfully, obediently, and even biblically as we may make our plans, it doesn't mean they will prevail (Proverbs 19:21), nor does failure of a plan necessarily mean it was a bad thing to work towards.

When we commit our plans to the Lord (Psalm 37:5), we sometimes assume that his blessing will follow as though our prayers are blueprints for our lives. What actually follows is surrender to a sovereign God, who takes into account much more than we could think to pray (Ephesians 3:20) in order to work good for us (Romans 8:28).

Our challenge is to get better at responding to a God who doesn't function according to our scripts. It doesn't mean we don't pray and seek and walk in a particular direction, but that we become more adaptable to the tweaks and adjustments that arise along the way, growing less stressed when we have to shift gears mid-journey.

The story of Abraham is an excellent example of this type of surrendered faith (Genesis 15–22). After what we can only imagine were years of begging God for children (sound familiar?), and years of trying to achieve this blessing on his own terms and his own way (sound more familiar?), Abraham finally received the son he had been promised by God.

But shortly thereafter, God asked Abraham to sacrifice his son. Abraham commenced in obedience. Then, at what seemed the last possible moment, God intervened and provided a way to spare Isaac's life and affirm Abraham's faith.

This sounds pretty barbaric to the modern ear, but we soon learn that this was a test of faith, a validation of God's good intention despite the means by which it unfolded. The comfort of obedience comes from knowing that whatever happens will always come with God's provision and strength. The point isn't about whether God would give Abraham a son, or even whether he would take his son away; the point is whether Abraham would trust God's plan.

For the single person, the point isn't whether God brings you a spouse. The point is, do you trust his plan? Are you surrendered to his will? Can you lay your hopes on the altar and trust him with the result? Will you obey regardless? Can you accept his comfort and strength to deal with whatever comes?

In giving my life to the Lord, I can be surprised about when he actually takes it, especially when it seems to be in a direction I did not ask for. But he knows how easy it is for me to confuse the plans I hope for with the purpose he has promised. He knows the foundation that is needed to build the life he has for me. He knows how to prioritize the many prayers I fire heavenward, and that the "how" I beg him for, may actually be standing in the way of the "what" he knows I really desire.

I see God's sovereignty as a spiritual tension, almost like a two-sided coin. A God of great power—whose plans are already written for me (Psalm 139:16), who works all things together for my good (Romans 8:28), lights my path (Psalm 119:105), and orders my steps (Psalm 37:23)—still allows me to have free will. My decisions have an impact, from reaping what I sow (Galatians 6:7) to my prayer having influence (James 5:16) to my words having the power of life and death (Proverbs 18:21). Perhaps Jesus is taking the wheel, but he still expects my foot to be on the gas.

When it comes to unwanted singleness, it's easier to feel like a victim and blame God when I'm unhappy than to admit I might have responsibilities in that unhappiness. I typically do this in a quasi-fatalistic way under the guise of trusting his sovereignty. I say things like, "If God wanted me to be married, I would be." There may even be some truth to such a statement, but it limits the many plans and answers God has for me. I think the Holy Spirit can absolutely set up the timing of romantic relationships and draw people together. I believe that a heavenly Father who knows how many hairs are on my head (Luke 12:7) is certainly interested in my romantic relationships. But I'm cautious about attributing things to God's will that may very well be the fruit of my own decisions.

It's easy to champion free will when it leads to things we like, then blame God when the same will walks us into situations we find uncomfortable. It's also easy to migrate from desperately wanting and praying for something to thinking that God has promised it to us. And it's more likely that we will mishear, misinterpret, and misunderstand the word, will, and inspiration of God when we have tunnel vision about what we're asking him for. Too often we go to God with closed yes-or-no questions or an advanced idea of the kind of answers we'll accept. But what if we went to God and trusted him with possibilities? What if, in our asking, we acknowledged that he could have bigger and better ideas than what we might be able to pray?

I grew up with the story that my parents prayed over me and my future spouse while I was still in the womb. They would physically lay their hands on my mother's growing pregnant belly and lift my life and future marriage to God. What an amazing heritage to have!

For a long time, I took this to mean that I would for sure get married. How could I not with a prayer history like that? When I felt frustrated at my dating life, or concerned about the lack of available partners, I would just go back to that story and think, *God has someone for me.* I thought this was what was me trusting in God, but it was actually just being comforted by the thought of him doing what I wanted him to do.

A god that can fit inside my head is no God at all. Just because someone prays something doesn't mean it will come true. In fact, a perfectly acceptable response to a prayer is "No." And just because God says no doesn't mean the prayer was bad. Prayers aren't wishes rubbed out of a magic lamp. God is not a genie or fairy godmother; he is a father who invites us all to a powerful and ongoing dialogue. We pray to him because he is sovereign, and we pray to him because our voice matters, and the seeming disparity between those two things never goes away.

The distinction I've had to wrestle with is whether I see myself as part of God's story or see him as part of mine. I think it's both, but it's a matter of emphasis. For years, the church depicted God as part of our story, with the moment of salvation being described as inviting Jesus into our hearts. But as long as God is positioned as part of my story, I will wrestle with why he hasn't brought the plot and actors together according to my preferred narrative. Once I place myself in the grand picture of everything God is doing, my gaze shifts, my focus changes, and the marriage stuff starts to feel a bit small by comparison.

I am working on trusting God and his goodness more by being less curious about who God may or may not have for me to marry and more curious about what God has for me to do while I'm on earth. I'm learning to follow the example of my Creator by being as innovative, inspired, and industrious as possible with what he has put before me. I am joining him in creating an amazing story.

Living in the will of God isn't always easy. Most of us would prefer the life of resurrection without the self-denial of the cross. This pursuit of faith, this surrender of our plans, can sometimes feel like a death, because it is. While we don't need to physically die to gain access to God's favour and grace, we do need his strength to put our earthly natures to death (Colossians 3:5), take up our crosses (Luke 9:23), and lay down our lives (Romans 12:1). This is why James instructs us to grieve, mourn and wail as part of humbling ourselves before a God who lifts us up (James 4:9–10). This path to freedom is counterintuitive, but it's in this kind of death that we truly gain (Philippians 1:21), because it forces us to let go of all the trappings, counterfeits, and crutches of faux freedom and rely on the one who can give us unending life.

In these moments of grief, it is common to doubt God, or at least to doubt that he is good. This puts us in good company. Even Jesus's closest friends, who saw him die and later walk among them, still doubted him (Matthew 28:17).

God can handle our doubts, and we need not resolve them all to move forward in faith. To think God has forsaken you and feel daunted by the sacrifice he demands is to resonate with Christ's humanity. To trust that God will rescue you and then commit your destiny to him is to affiliate with Christ's faith. Following Jesus has tremendous blessings, but it is a way of sacrifice. What do we expect taking up our cross to practically look like if not the daily offering of our preferences and desires? What do we think a surrendered life will be if not one where we lay our dreams *of* an altar *on* the altar? Where do we think a life modelled after a sacrificial lamb will take us if not to a deep reckoning of wills.

It is terrifying to observe what God seems to permit and comforting to recall that he is in control, frustrating that he answers our prayers in ways we wish he wouldn't and gobsmacking that he answers them at all. I don't think that wrestling (Genesis 32:22–32) with God ever fully ends; rather, it's part of the working out of our salvation (Philippians 2:12). God isn't far-off in these moments. He doesn't leave or forsake (Deuteronomy 31:6) us or get tired of our doubts and wonderings. In fact, he wants to be in the struggle with us. God is both the roaring lion of Judah (Revelation 5:5) and the still small voice (1 Kings 19:12). He is both a consuming fire (Hebrews 12:29) and never-ending love (1 John 4:8). His sovereignty means that we cannot predict him, but his faithfulness means that we can always rely on him. His methods may not be safe, but his power makes us secure.

I don't know if I will marry. And if I do, I don't know who I will marry. God's ability to transcend time and know such things right now doesn't eliminate my role in making my own choice. The lack of resolution doesn't exclude me from being accountable for how his ultimate commission, expressed scriptural promises, and clear directives play out in my life. One prayer request not going my way doesn't excuse a life of victimhood, staleness, and impatience towards God.

A dear friend of mine, now in her seventies, was widowed in her thirties. Though she desires companionship and has tried dating many times, she has never remarried. I once ventured to ask her about how she managed her forty years of singleness post-marriage, and over a long pot of tea I tried to drink in the wisdom she shared. At some point, the conversation came around to how she viewed God in light of the ache that could sometimes be in her heart. Her response was powerful: "It's not God's job to bring us someone. It's God's job to love us."

I don't always know which choices are mine and which are God's, but I trust him enough to keep working it out. I want to continue pursuing him, not just for what I think he can do for me. While I might not always understand his ways, it is my privilege to know his love.

PART THREE

LEARN HOW TO BE A
Person

PART THREE

THE BIBLE IS FOR ME: CONFESSIONS OF AN ACCIDENTAL FEMINIST

Our deepest fear is not that we are inadequate. Our deepest fear is that we are powerful beyond measure. It is our light, not our darkness that most frightens us. We ask ourselves, "Who am I to be brilliant, gorgeous, talented, fabulous?" Actually, who are you not to be? You are a child of God. Your playing small does not serve the world. There is nothing enlightened about shrinking so that other people won't feel insecure around you. We are all meant to shine, as children do. We were born to make manifest the glory of God that is within us. It's not just in some of us; it's in everyone. And as we let our own light shine, we unconsciously give other people permission to do the same. As we are liberated from our own fear, our presence automatically liberates others.[26]
—Marianne Williamson

"ARE YOU A feminist?"

Asked a voice from two seats over on the plane. The tone, whether accusatory or curious, signalled an abrupt end to a daydream that had me lagging behind the conversation of my travel companions.

The question seemed pointed and blunt, mostly because it was the first time I had been asked it in such a long time. From previously working in a church in a conservative region to working in higher education in a decidedly progressive part of the country, the question of feminism was seldom raised because the answer, however varied, was usually a foregone conclusion. I was usually content to allow the answer to be implied. This saved arguments, politicking, and conversational energy best reserved for less incendiary topics.

But as I sipped from my dixie cup of ginger ale, I realized that the question's wallop wasn't due to its recency; it was the fact that it was the first time I had been asked directly since my answer has changed.

Because I am a Christian, I never thought of myself as a feminist. Strongly influenced by the evangelical circles in which I was raised, if feminism was a religion, then I was an atheist well into adulthood.

My first association with the word did not inspire womanly pride; in fact, it accomplished quite the opposite. The details are somewhat hazy, but I know I was about seven years old and an adult was changing the channel away from a news story about women protesting topless in the streets. Their faces were stern, their voices hoarse, their dialogue bleeped out, and their skin seemed goose-pimply as it was too cold to be out of doors without a jacket, much less a shirt. And they were undoubtedly angry. Just looking at them made me feel sad and confused.

I still don't know what they were protesting, but I remember every time I heard the word feminist after that day, I pictured those women—red-faced, bare-chested, foul-mouthed, and vibrating with hostility towards the men around them. And I remember deciding in all my seven-year-old wisdom that I would never, ever be one of them.

Perhaps it's a cautionary tale about first impressions, inadvertent insight into the waves of the feminist movement, or another piece of evidence for why we should never say never, but I was influenced and biased by my first exposure to the movement. I spent the better part of my youth and education defending an anti-feminist position. For a long time, I thought my traditional upbringing stood ideologically opposed to the general rhetoric and tenure of feminism. Like so many around me still do, I pictured angry, marching women and imagined that the word meant I had to be anti-family, anti-man, anti-marriage, anti-motherhood, pro-abortion, and against any gender norms in a relationship. Sure, I would claim the collective benefits of the movement—education, career options, owning property, voting, an independent chequing account, wearing pants—but I didn't want to be associated with all of *those* rebellious women.

What I didn't realize then was that my resistance to feminism was made of the same stuff that kept my life and perspective small. My anti-feminism was so wrapped up in my identity as a potential wife and future mother that it was easy for me to neglect all the other aspects of being a person, a woman, and a Christian.

Evangelical culture often mistakenly implies that the biblical instructions for wives and husbands are also intended for women and men in general. If you view marriage as guaranteed, and non-marriage as a state of preparation for marriage, it's a natural step to assume that any passing scriptural reference to a marital state is *for you*. For ages, men, women, aspiring theologians, and freshman Bible studies have been discussing the pitfalls and advantages of egalitarianism (men and women as non-hierarchical, equal partners with overlapping roles) and complementarianism (men and women as uniquely paired, with distinct roles and hierarchical expression) in a debate that never ends. Ever.

I don't remember with whom, but I was somewhere in the middle of another exhausting conversation about the topic when I had a freeing revelation: not having to be absolutely sure about this is one of the advantages of being single! Sure, a philosophy of gender politics in marriage might inform how I interact with married friends, but as for myself? I don't actually need to know how I'll get along with a husband right now, because I don't have one. I also don't need to know how I'll parent unless or until I'm parenting, just as I don't know how I'll grieve the death of a close friend until they die. I don't doubt the value of having some foreknowledge, skill, or opinion regarding these topics in service of being community-minded or emotionally intelligent, but after that they're just ideas.

I don't have to know how to love or honour a husband I don't have. I don't have to sort out who does the cooking and the housework and who does the accounting and handiwork. Since I live alone, I do everything.

So perhaps those verses aren't actually about me. While complementarianism and egalitarianism limit the discussion of who an individual is in relationship to members of their sex, the single person has the freedom to be more interested in who they are in relationship to Jesus.

When I stopped constantly conceptualizing my single life as premarital, I was confronted with the ridiculousness of how much time I had spent preparing to be a godly spouse rather than on actually being a godly person. How many hours had I needlessly rehashed minor points of gender theology rather than actually taking ground for the kingdom? How often had I viewed the stewardship of my purity as a gift for a future spouse rather than a path to God's will? How frequently had I overlooked scriptures that could apply to me because I didn't see them as being directed toward wives and mothers?

With clearer vision myself, it still astounds me how many formal Christian teachings and organizations encourage men to subjugate women and women to be smaller or lesser versions of themselves in order for the two to be compatible in marriage. This isn't only demeaning to women whose talents are buried; it's also demeaning to men who we presume won't have the capacity to handle us at full throttle. It's the kind of perversion of theology that animalizes men, objectifies women, and justifies sexualized violence in a rape culture that some argue is worse in traditional Christendom than in the secular world.

And all this supposedly in the name of biblical submission.

This begs the question: if a man never gets married, can he still be a complementarian? I don't think so. All women aren't called to submit to all men; wives are called to submit to their husbands and husbands to sacrificially love their wives, and in fact we're all called to submit to each other in general (Ephesians 5:21–33). I have ideas about what submission means, but the point is that this passage doesn't have much to do with the everydayness of my singlehood. It seems a shame that rather than holding up the sacrifice required for marriage as one reason that singleness might be a preferable state, to have instead spent my singleness preparing for the sacrifice.

If I get married someday, I'll have to learn how to cooperate in a marriage relationship. I will need the help of the others and the Holy Spirit to do so, and I'll most likely have some time dating and being engaged to prepare me for that. But until then, or if that never happens, what does it matter? And even if it does matter, isn't the best preparation I can undertake to be living fully for God right now? How lazy will my submission be if I've kept my life so small and codependent that I have nothing to submit? How weak will my love be if I fail to live to my full potential so I'll have less to sacrifice in the event of a union? How naïve am I to think that any surrendered life won't at some point involve sacrifice of my personal preferences for the sake of something or someone greater?

I serve a God big enough to give me a vision for my life in or outside of a marriage relationship. I no longer consternate over whether I'm allowed to use my gifts, or worry about whether this will make me seem too intimidating to men. I don't fuss about how I'll stifle my talents for the sake of marital unity someday. I also no longer put pressure on every man I meet to be "spiritual leader" material. I'm too busy serving Jesus to indulge a malnourished theology of marriage that requires two supposedly Christ-filled people to remain stagnant and timid in order to get along later.

Once I broke free from thinking of my life as a perpetual training ground for marriage, my views on marriage seemed a lot less important, my views on feminism became a lot more important, and my walk with Christ became a lot more free. Since I've stopped reading the scriptures about marriage as if they apply to everyone all the time, I have more time to read the many more scriptures that apply to every other aspect of life. I'm more focused on being the leader God has called me to be than worrying about how I might submit to a spiritual leader husband someday or whether that's even a thing. I'm less interested in making myself small, cooperative, and domestic and more focused on letting my light shine.

This can seem adversarial to those who still think all women should submit to all men, but I can love those people without agreeing with them. This can be threatening to those still trying to earn marriage by being ready enough for it, but I'm personally ready to let that fight go.

Around the time I was figuring this out, I had lunch with a Christian colleague. A statement she made crystalized these thoughts for me. I confessed that I thought I was becoming a feminist, less for the label and more in response to a call—to stand in the gap for the oppressed, to advocate for those still stuck in an old dichotomy, to champion freedom for women deceived into an identity dependent on men, and to influence men to realize that it's not weak to be inspired by godly women.

"Exactly," she answered. "I'm a feminist *because* I'm a Christian, not in spite of it!"

Being open to such possibilities gives me fresh perspective on the things I thought I knew. For example, I've encountered many stories about the supposed crisis of single women in the modern church. These commentaries about the pitiful unmarried women over thirty sitting in church pews are usually followed by instructions to convene in prayer that God would work in new ways to provide husbands for these women. But this doesn't account for the emerging research telling us that some of the happiest people on earth are single and child-free women.[27] In fact, for centuries women have been seeking God for independence, promotion, leadership, opportunity, open doors, and ultimately freedom. Yet now there are scores of women in our churches who have received exactly those gifts, but instead are begging God for husbands and families and the traditional path. What if God is just answering the prayers of centuries of women before us? What if he is trying to continue a revolution and we're too busy calling it a crisis of singleness to notice?

The truth is that my embrace of feminism has allowed me to be a much happier and more effective single person. I've been led to see Christ as a life-maker, not a wife-maker. It took some left-leaning momentum to rock me, not away from my core values but towards Jesus.

How had I read the Bible for so long without realizing how much it had to say to me about things other than marriage and parenting? How had I attended church my whole life and not felt the empowerment that Jesus offered women?

I started to wonder whether the spaces between the extremes of the feminism I thought I knew and the traditionalism I thought I needed were revealing to me an alternate way of being in the world. Did I have to choose, or could I have both a passion for Jesus and a gift for leading others to him? An interest in family and a capable and fulfilling career and single life? A more conservative sexual ethic and a fiery feminist advocacy? Could I be the strong, independent woman God seemed to be asking me to be, whether or not he ever brought a husband into my picture? Did I have to let go of my desire for an equally strong man to partner with someday? Could I serve in, submit to, and embrace the church with the love of Christ while disagreeing about so many of the ways it behaves regarding gender? These are questions I'm willing to ask now. They are shaping me into a better person. And yeah, if I get married someday, I'm guessing they will help me to be a much more thoughtful, integral, and powerful wife.

Sometimes I wish I had a new word for feminism, something that could embody everything it means to be a Holy-Spirit-led woman without everything else that gets associated with the term. I wish I could somehow detach the calling that has awoken in me from the ideology I don't unwaveringly cling to.

But, I realize that my ability to even discuss such things in a public forum is due to all the things the word has meant over time, and all the women and men who did my dirty work for me, fighting battles in corners I would have left dark.

I could say the exact same of the word Christian, a word with so many interpretations and so much baggage that I wish the first mental picture in someone's head, when I disclose I am one, wasn't everything they hate about conservatives.

But I need both words. I need the history, injustice, hypocrisy, vulnerability, and sacrifice that make them nuanced, misunderstood, and messy. I stand humbly among the shattered glass of ceilings broken above me by courageous women and men whose bodies were scarred with the shards of dogma and whose hearts were alive with the song of a Saviour who knows what it is to shed blood for freedom.

"Are you a feminist?"

The question hung in midair. I felt a tingle in my spine and a flutter in my stomach, as if I was about to profess my faith in some new way.

If you want to start a conversation that will last a six-hour flight, just ask an accidental feminist about her conversion story.

"Yes," I stated plainly. I was confident and wanted to be neither defensive nor evangelistic.

"Why?"

This follow-up sounded more of a challenge than a point of curiosity, I thought. I inhaled as I pondered the wisdom of many gut-wrenching years.

"Because I'm a Christian…"

FOLLOWING THE LEADER: HOW JESUS DID SINGLENESS

For we do not have a high priest who is unable to sympathize with our weaknesses, but one who in every respect has been tempted as we are, yet without sin. Let us then with confidence draw near to the throne of grace, that we may receive mercy and find grace to help in time of need.
(Hebrews 4:15–16, ESV)

ONCE YOU'VE HONOURED your grief, acknowledged your sexual self, figured out that it's okay to be single, and stopped thinking of marriage as being inevitable, it turns out there is a lot of living to do.

But the question of how to do that isn't always straightforward, and advice can be lacking. Single adults are just as responsible for living well as coupled adults; they may just have less help figuring out how to do it.

For me, discerning a way forward started when I changed the filter I was listening through and sought advice, wisdom, examples, and instruction on how to just be an adult: how to communicate, deal with loneliness, address selfishness, manage money, and more. Not only did I find several varied and indirect sources of instruction, but I also began to connect with my Saviour in a whole new way.

Singles are frequently directed to look at the life of Paul as an example of singleness, but we often neglect a more significant example: Christ himself.

It's interesting to me that as Christians we encourage one another to look to Jesus's example for indications of how to do life in so many areas, yet we seldom reference his methodology for living as a single person. Good news: Jesus was single! That means we have both the example and compassion of a Saviour who has been there.

Though some may dismiss Jesus's example of singleness as the choice of someone who was fully God (Colossians 2:9), they may overlook that he was also fully human (John 1:14), which means we can't just dismiss his singleness with a flippant, "Yeah, but he was God, so it doesn't count." In some ways, it counts more.

Jesus entered a human world steeped in longstanding religious mythology filled with gods who often pursued their own romantic dalliances and attempted to satisfy every sexual urge. It would therefore have been significant for God to choose singleness in his human form. Being fully human means Jesus was a living, breathing, vulnerable, arousable being with deep desires for connection, companionship, and intimacy. Yet we also know that he was without fault (1 Peter 2:22), so in being human, he did not sin.

The fact that Jesus was Jewish means he would have grown up immersed in traditional teachings including the concepts of finding a suitable helpmate and producing children to fill the earth. Yet somehow he navigated his life managing the theological tension between marriage and singleness. He embodied the value of both, using marriage as the metaphor to describe his relationship with the church while choosing to be single himself. Though we have reason to believe Jesus wasn't exceptionally good-looking (Isaiah 53:2), the fact that he was wise and kind, an effective public speaker, a healer, and capable of drawing a crowd means it was likely that several of his many followers would have seen him as a desirable romantic partner, and they possibly indicated so in their attentions. After all, they thought they were interacting with the next king.

So when we're told that he was exposed to every temptation (Hebrews 4:15) we can be sure to include romantic allurements and seduction on the list.

We cannot dismiss Jesus's response, or lack thereof, to these temptations as some impossible standard set by the divine, as he himself said that we would do greater things than him (John 14:12). While God deems that it's not good for man to be alone (Genesis 2:18), Jesus showed us that it could be good for one to be single.

Our Saviour is more than the one who comforts us in our singleness. He is an example of how to do it, and do it well.

So how did Jesus do it?

HE CONNECTED INTIMATELY AND CONTINUOUSLY WITH THE FATHER

An obvious answer that bubbles to the surface about how Jesus led a purposeful single life was his constant and intimate connection with God the Father. Jesus constantly prioritized time alone, and time in prayer. When facing challenges to his character or ministry, he could quote scripture cold, which means he also prioritized time in study. He could call out others for being of little faith because he knew what it meant to live a life of faith himself. He modelled the way of worship by living a life laid out in service to God's will.

No thriving single life will be possible without this type of devotion, because to live the life a single is called to is to require the grace and power of the Holy Spirit. Spending time with God in prayer, the reading of scripture, and the communion of fellowship are all important. These practices are what it looks like to remain connected to God as the source (John 15:4).

One reason connection with God is so important is that it allows for a continuous affirmation of identity. When Jesus was challenged, tempted, and pained, as he was in the desert (Matthew 4:1–11) and the Garden of Gethsemane (Mathew 26:36–46), his identity was affirmed through his connection with the Father and his knowledge of the scriptures.

Challenges to our identities are frequent. When we're stigmatized or rejected on account of our singleness, or when our sense of worth takes a hit in light of our dating lives, it's important that we can refresh our understanding of who we are in the Father's eyes.

HE WAS ON A MISSION

Jesus had a mission in coming to earth and it shaped everything he did from a young age. Even at twelve years old, he positioned himself as a curious learner, staying behind in the temple after the family pilgrimage to Jerusalem to seek wisdom and knowledge from his elders and teachers (Luke 2:41-50). He knew that he was positioned to do his Father's work, and he publicly self-identified with Isaiah's prophecy:

> The Spirit of the Lord is on me, because he has anointed me to proclaim good news to the poor. He has sent me to proclaim freedom for the prisoners and recovery of sight for the blind, to set the oppressed free, to proclaim the year of the Lord's favor. (Luke 4:18–19)

Jesus came to seek and save the lost, restore peace in the community, destroy the works of the devil, establish a republic of love, call and make disciples, and bring both the event and process of reconciliation.

In Mark Buchanan's words, he came to find whatever wasn't working and do good works to rescue those involved from their bondage.[28]

This mission is what guarded Jesus from temptation. It's what gave him grace and patience in leading a team of often bafoony disciples. It allowed him to prioritize little children over religious expectations, spiritual depth above political manoeuvring, and gave him courage in the face of certain death.

As Christ followers, we join in this mission too. How we carry it out in our own lives and communities will be different for each of us, but the same principles of love, reconciliation, redemption, and discipleship apply. Discovering how the great commission plays out in our personal missions is part of the beauty and journey of life and can be an anchor to a single person looking for meaning and fulfillment.

Mission brings a sense of purpose to life that transcends relationship status. Mission is the filter by which we determine our values, choose our relationships, and select our activities. It's what helps decide what work we take on, what service we engage with, and what hobbies fill our time.

Mission also helps us decide what not to do.

A clear mission may not be easy, but it makes decisions simple. While morals and values can help us decide between good and bad, mission helps us discern between multiple possible good things.

A compelling mission is intrinsically motivating. While being missional doesn't mean you'll never wrestle with God's plan—since even Jesus prayed for God to relieve him of the task at hand (Luke 22:42)—it will give you the focus, strength, and courage to live out that plan.

I remember hearing a Bible camp sermon about King David, the same David who killed Goliath when he was just a shepherd boy. The preacher made an important connection: the reason David had been able to face Goliath and King Saul was that he already knew he would be king (1 Samuel 16–24). David had been anointed to the kingship at such a young age that he lived fearlessly with an attitude that assured him, "I can't die yet because I'm not yet king. This won't overtake me because I haven't finished what I'm here to do."

The same theme can be found in many other stories throughout the Bible.

Noah faced the ridicule of his peers. He spent more than a hundred years building the Ark because he knew God had called him to rescue humanity from a flood.

Queen Esther faced King Xerxes and the possibility of death because her mission to save her people was more powerful than her fear.

Paul faced prison, shipwrecks, and personal beatings because he knew that calling others to salvation and discipleship was worth any cost. His life also serves as an example of how singleness can be an advantage when considering the potential peril of mission: he could volunteer for any kingdom assignment, regardless of the danger it presented, knowing he would leave nobody fatherless or spouseless.

David could face Goliath because he knew his mission. Esther could face the king because she knew her mission. Jesus could face the cross because he knew his mission.

You can face singleness when you know your mission. Furthermore, you can embrace your singleness when you know it's part of how you are to carry out the great commission. There doesn't need to be a reason for your singleness, but you can use your singleness for good reasons.

Once I truly saw my singleness as a gift, it naturally fell into the same category as other riches with which I'd been entrusted—and it soon demanded the same response of stewardship.

The scriptural concept of stewardship comes with a few assumptions:

- What we have is not ours but a gift from God.
- We have a choice, authority, and responsibility over how we spend God's gifts.
- We are accountable for those choices.

I think this is why so many people connect the dots between being single and being in ministry.

Those who try to embrace the concept of singleness as a gift will ask me, "Do you think you're single so that you can be in ministry?" I usually answer "Sort of," or a provisional yes. I agree that God is using my singleness for his glory, but I think most people define ministry far too narrowly.

I think that many people are confused about their mission. They're begging God to know why they're single when they don't feel "called to ministry" and are at a loss because they have incorrectly defined what ministry is.

But as Pat Lencioni says, "all work is ministry."[29] Ministry is not reserved for professional Christians who decide to work in churches, missions, and faith-based nonprofits. While ministry can fall into more traditional catchments such as worship, kids, teens, and men's and women's programs, it's not reserved for what happens in church organizations or limited to age, relationship status, or gender-specific tasks in a specific community. The single person can take heart: there is more for them to contribute to the kingdom than volunteering in the kids ministry, hanging out with other singles, or heading overseas.

Ministry is about mission, seeing the purposes of God in whatever you do. As a Christian, you are a minister of the gospel wherever you go. Ministry is not a specific career path, volunteer experience, or relationship arrangement; it's an entire way of interacting with the world. Whether you're at work, at play, or at home, you are in and preparing for ministry. Whether you serve food, sell clothes, write computer code, crunch numbers, teach literature, build houses, dig ditches, legally defend, artistically portray, medically diagnose, serve, protect, or something else, you are in ministry. Whether single or coupled, our lives are for ministry: to work at whatever we do as an act of worship for him and love for others (1 Corinthians 10:31), mindful of our kingdom influence, looking for strategic linkages and prepared to give an answer for our hope (1 Peter 3:15).

What may be a single's advantage in this universal Christian mission, is the undivided attention they can devote to such an assignment. It is true that my brain isn't currently occupied with romance, marital relationship growth, childrearing, or the daily considerations expected when sharing money and domestic responsibility with others. I have comparatively more time and energy to spend contemplating and praying for myself and the people and issues I am connected to, and more freedom to make choices without negotiating or waiting for a partner to get on the same page.

This advantage was poignantly demonstrated when I was pursuing a graduate degree. While I often sense God's prompting, I don't commonly perceive it in some kind of flashy, obvious way. But my decision to go to grad school was crystalized in a moment that brought me the closest I've ever come to hearing an audible voice from God. It was almost an out-loud instruction. And I didn't have to consult anyone. Granted, I have parents, siblings, mentors, friends, and coworkers who were all impacted in small ways—and I did speak with them, as I believe that there is wisdom in the multitude of counsel (Proverbs 11:14)—but I didn't need anyone's agreement, permission, or clearance to say yes. I didn't have to convince someone that it was okay to take on a financially gargantuan commitment without being certain of how I would pay for it. I didn't have to negotiate over how much time I would spend at work and on my computer for the next four years. I didn't have to consider what it would mean for someone else's eating, sleeping, cleaning, or social schedule or what their schedule might mean for my ability to complete a thesis. I didn't have to convince someone that I had heard from the Holy Spirit.

I just said yes.

Even outside of faith-based considerations, one can celebrate mission and the independence to move their lives forward in a single state.

I have a friend who considers herself a serial monogamist. She has been in several two- to three-year relationships in her life, with gaps in between. Her comment to me was that she has always moved her life forward the most—such as in terms of education, career, and finances—when she has been single.

Steven Covey's oft-cited "big rock demonstration" illustrates that personal effectiveness stems from prioritizing one's time and energy by putting first things first: setting the most important aspects of our lives (big rocks) first and filling in the gaps with the remainder of what matters in descending order of importance (little rocks, gravel, etc.).[30]

The takeaway is that one can fit a lot into life if everything is correctly prioritized. Even at my busiest and most productive, as a single, I have at least one more big rock space than most of my peers, as I don't need to assign a rock to a romantic relationship, and still another when I consider that I'm not a parent. I'm learning to value this space and see it as a privilege and something to be stewarded.

The scriptural parallel to this is the concept of putting God first and allowing everything else to fall in line (Matthew 6:33). It's easier to put God first when there isn't someone else in our lives competing for the same attention.

This is what it means when I say that part of how I use my singleness is for ministry. It doesn't necessarily mean that I spend every day in hours of prayer, scripture study, and fasting or that I feel called to lead or plant a church or a mission at this time, though for some it may. At a higher level it means I have the liberty to follow Christ and come up with crazy fun adventurous ideas without being concerned about how they'll impact a romantic partnership and lifelong covenant.

As a side note, just because God may have given you extra time and space to fulfill your role in his mission doesn't mean that the mission will be inside your comfort zone. In fact, he may very well stretch you beyond your limits so you'll have to rely on the Holy Spirit to accomplish what he has set out for you to do. The God who doesn't fit inside my head calls me to a life that won't stay within my control, which demands an ability only he can provide.

What if your singleness is a resource God has given you? What if it's part of how he wants you to fulfill your part in the great commission? What do you have access to, resources for, and freedom in that could move your life and the kingdom of God forward here on earth in a unique way? How are you taking responsibility for the advantages with which God has entrusted you? This type of opportunity is much more significant than a flippant comment like "You're single in order to be in ministry." It's a weighty responsibility of discretionary time, resources, and energy that could be spent in a myriad of ways.

I sometimes imagine a future conversation in heaven where I ask God why he didn't give me the chance to be a spouse or raise a family as a young adult, and he responds by asking me what I did with all that non-spousing and non-parenting time. If we ever have that conversation, I want to be able to answer him with something more significant than a series of bad online dates, my Netflix queue, my social media feeds, and the list of qualities I was praying for in a partner.

I don't think singles are more responsible to live well than married people, but I think we have unique responsibilities in living well that may not apply to those who are busy fostering a marriage or raising the next generation. And I don't mean to imply that singles aren't busy, because caring and providing for ourselves, cultivating community, and possibly seeking family still take up time and energy. I'm just saying that I now see privileges in the single life and I'm trying not to waste them.

The faith I'm learning to share is one that holds good news for everyone, including the single. Good news! You don't need a romantic relationship to define you. You can live a purposeful, missional, fulfilling life right now. Regardless of romance, you can have love, community, connection, intimacy, and adventure.

This gospel extends to so many who have traversed a traditional relationship status only to find themselves in evangelical no man's land. Good news, divorcée: you haven't committed the unpardonable sin. Good news, single parent: he is a Father to the fatherless. Good news, widow or widower: the family of God is here to care for you. Good news, empty nester: God isn't done with you yet. Good news, married person: your relationship doesn't have to be perfect or meet all your needs.

HE CHANGED THE DEFINITION OF FAMILY

It doesn't take a significant amount of Bible scholarship to realize that Jesus was a relational guy. We have specific accounts of him investing in relationships with the disciples and his friends. Perhaps he, Mary, Martha, and Lazarus even bonded over being single.

Besides these connections, he travelled around with a constant posse, stood against social injustice, brought healing and freedom to many, frequently demonstrated and taught the importance and merits of loving others, scoffed at religiosity, bureaucracy and barriers to human intimacy, metaphorically depicted the church as his bride, and then gave up his life for the world.

Even in his constant pursuit of relationships, Jesus challenged the status quo. For him, marriage and family were temporary constructs that served as metaphors for community. They were the symbol that had forecasted his work to ultimately unite himself with the church. While he upheld the honouring of parents (Matthew 15:4), the valuing of children (Matthew 19:14), and the unity of marriage (Matthew 19:1–11), he wasn't stuck in the mentality that biological linkages were superior to community and connection. He often spoke of traditional family ties as a barrier to kingdom living (Matthew 10:34–39, Matthew 19:29, Luke 14:26) yet invited all who would come into the family of God through the adoption he would purchase on the cross (Romans 8:16).

Jesus demonstrated that while connection, community, and relationships are all very important, they don't have to fit the label of family that we're used to. Even in taking care of his own mother upon his death, he did so by entrusting her care to a nonbiological connection (John 19:25–27).

Jesus taught us to pray that God's kingdom would come as it is in heaven (Matthew 6:9–13). The implications of this for marriage and family are interesting when we consider that marriage doesn't survive death (Matthew 22:30, Romans 7:2). The kind of family that extends beyond eternity must have a different look and feel than what we may be used to.

> While Jesus was still talking to the crowd, his mother and brothers stood outside, wanting to speak to him. Someone told him, "Your mother and brothers are standing outside, wanting to speak to you."
>
> He replied to him, "Who is my mother, and who are my brothers?" Pointing to his disciples, he said, "Here are my mother and my brothers.

> For whoever does the will of my Father in heaven is my brother and sister and mother." (Matthew 12:46–50)

In the kingdom Jesus modelled, anyone pursuing the will of God is family! He gave his blood to open the door to a new definition of love, relationship, and inclusion. In doing so, he ushered in a new covenant.

But this new covenant, requires a new understanding of almost everything, and we get confused when we mix components of Jewish law with modern Christendom in a Jesus-plus[31] hybrid that is less than the full freedom Christ promised.

The old covenant model of family was a microcosm, or foreshadowing, of what would be possible under the new command of Christ. Faith, justification, sanctification, and multiplication are all still core to the recipe, but they have a different flavour in a new covenant world.

For example, we are no longer bound to the law of tithing a percentage of our income to God (Leviticus 27:30) but instead to cheerful giving (2 Corinthians 9), consistent generosity, and stewardship of all that we have for the sake of the kingdom. We are no longer required to sacrifice animals or observe rituals to atone for our state of having fallen short of God's holiness (Exodus 20:24). Instead we participate in the communion that reminds us of Christ's ultimate sacrifice of death (1 Corinthians 11:23–25). We are no longer subjected to the act of circumcision to identify as one of God's people (Genesis 17:11) but instead baptised into his death and resurrection (Romans 6:3-4). Our worship is no longer comprised of the songs we perform inside the structure of a temple building (1 Chronicles 6:32); it is a living sacrifice (Romans 12:1) of continuous praise (Hebrews 13:15) by one who is the temple of the Holy Spirit (1 Corinthians 6:19). Where a family was begun through a man and woman joining and becoming one flesh (Genesis 2:24), we now join the existing family of God by becoming one with Christ himself (Romans 6:5).

COMPONENTS OF FAITH	OLD COVENANT EXPRESSION	NEW COVENANT EXPRESSION
Giving	Tithing	Stewardship and generosity
Recognition of justification	Animal sacrifice	Communion
Identification as God's people	Circumcision	Baptism
Worship	Temple acts	Daily commitment
Family	Biological	Spiritual

The covenant shift for family is both significant and neglected. The first command God gave creation, both before and after the flood, was to be fruitful and multiply (Genesis 1:28, Genesis 9:7), and the first expression of the old covenant with Abraham was that God would greatly increase his numbers (Genesis 17:2), but the parting commission of a resurrected Christ to his followers was *"go and make disciples"* (Matthew 28:19).

Multiplication is still God's intention, but the method shifts under the new covenant from one of population to one of transformation, from one of making heirs to one of making followers. This was, and is to this day, a powerful, uncomfortable, and provocative upending of traditional family values, first to the Jews and then to the evangelicals. In this flipped emphasis, marriage is not wrong, but it's no longer considered the default. Singleness is the default, with marriage being the exception or the act of opting out of the norm of singleness.

How much less energy would the modern church need to spend on defending the integrity of marriage and the family if we truly believed this? Why would we settle for the symbol when we can have the real thing?

The church as depicted in the first few chapters of Acts is a poignant example of this new vision of family.

Monica Geyen and Rosaria Butterfield discussed it this way:

> Once upon a time, the church was *"of one heart and soul, and no one said that any of the things*

that belonged to him was his own, but they had everything in common," (Acts 4:32). Shared time, shared food, shared possessions. Shared identity. They were the early church — a family bound together by the blood of Jesus.[32]

The early movement of Jesus-followers recognized that regardless of relationship status, what makes a family—shared vision, mutual care, edification, communal resources, discipleship—transcends genetic and eternal boundaries. The values and responsibilities of family are upheld, but the duties are dispersed amongst many. We are to take care of each other, especially those whose nuclear families are not there to do so (1 Timothy 5:3–16). In this way, all people—including orphans, widows (James 1:27), and dare I say singles and never-marrieds—may have a place to belong through the entrance of faith.

This new definition of family can help the single to differentiate from their family of origin much more easily. Differentiation is a term from family therapy that describes a type of boundary-setting. It's the concept of being fully yourself even when in the presence of your family, who may tempt you towards old patterns of behaviour. It means the you who has intentionally learned ways of managing—money, conflict, health and otherwise—that differ from your upbringing, can return to a familial environment and hold its own. It links well with the original root word of alone, of being all one, or literally "wholly oneself."[33]

In a family that is a mixture of Christian expression and Judeo heritage, this can be tricky. Married couples have a clear line to cross, one that states, "We're a family now." It's linked to the idea of a man and woman leaving their families, uniting, and becoming one flesh (Genesis 2:24). Some couples manage to do this in their early days of marriage while others may need the buffer of children to help them. Still others struggle long into their marriages.

But eventually there is a point when a couple pushes back against the norms of their nuclear families and decides how their own household is going to function.

Can there or should there be a similar moment for the single person? If a person never marries, or is never given away in marriage, when do they become the head of their own household? Where is the rite of passage, the cord-cutting that leads to independence?

I would posit that for the single, and really for the new covenant Christian, that line is crossed when we surrender to Christ. For the parent wondering about when they release their child into the blessing of God's will, I am inclined to place the moment further from the handing of the bride to the groom at the end of the aisle, and closer to the ceremony of dedicating or christening that child to the Lord's service shortly after birth.

I'm not advocating for parent-child disunity, though. In fact, I think singles are often judged harshly and unfairly for remaining close to their families. But I don't believe a marriage is required for a person to individuate.

There will always be an imperative to honour family, as well as blessings that result from such honour, but my parentage need not stand in the way of my priesthood (1 Peter 2:5). In other words, not even my flesh and blood should ever come between me and God, nor should it dictate how I serve or am directed by him (Luke 9:60–62). We need not rely on a spouse, biological children, or earthly fathers to allow Christ himself to assert authority over how our lives are run.

Married or not, as for me and my house we can serve the Lord (Joshua 24:15). We also need not limit the love and support we give and receive to just those to whom we are biologically connected.

In the context of this broader family of God, we can both give and receive, teach and learn, love and be loved. In such a family, we can find the nourishment of friendship, the instruction of mentorship, and the correction of discipleship. Here we may benefit from the wisdom of age and the inspiration of youth. Here we can find physical affection, emotional validation, outlets for our gifts, and sources for our needs. Nobody is off the hook or outside the circle. All generations are part of the family of God, and each person has their own responsibilities.

What great news this would be for the suffering of our day and age, if we could fully express this version of family in our generation. This perspective may challenge our understandings of family ties, but if embraced it can give hope to the single person who wonders how they will find support, feedback, provision, and partnership outside of marriage, and care in their old age. It provides so much freedom, especially around the holidays, to adult singles who are more likely to find community or chosen family in friend groups.

Considering ourselves as part of the family of God may also provide some insight into how singles who aren't parents are to respond to the desire to have children. The pressure to procreate can be both biologically and sociologically intense, whether for the man who is socialized to continue the family line or the woman whose biological clock is ticking.

I have always desired to be a mother and assumed that children and coupledom would go together. But as I've aged, I've wondered if the two need necessarily be linked. While a secular perspective would say they don't, what is the Christian approach to the concept of optional single parenting?

I believe children are a blessing from God regardless of how they are brought into the world, and I don't think the desire for or pursuit of parenthood is wrong. But I do think it's easy to consider finding a way to have kids in order to meet a need in me, rather than allowing God to meet my needs in his way. If I want a baby to fill a hole in my heart, then I'm back to the same issues I had with wanting a partner, right?

It's also easy to underestimate the amount of work and sacrifice that go into parenting, especially single parenting, and to overlook how the responsibility might detract from other blessings or privileges of singleness. The question I've asked myself is this: will pursuing parenthood support my contentment as a single or make me further begrudge my solo state?

Many spiritual, moral, ethical, emotional, financial, and physical considerations go into the choice to single-parent, whether one is considering IVF, fostering, or adoption. Ultimately, I think this is one of those topics for which we need to seek the Holy Spirit's wisdom. Regardless of whether a single person already has children, brings children into the world, adopts children, or is wrestling with parental desires, the family of God will be part of any healthy equation.

The broader point is that we aren't limited to biological connection to meet our emotional needs under Jesus's definition of family. Seeing myself as part of the family of God means I don't need to be an actual mother or father to have a parental influence in the lives of children. I don't have to be biologically connected to the kids whom I love, spoil, and adore.

As a sidenote, this doesn't necessarily mean that singles everywhere want to be considered free babysitters, petsitters, and housesitters. We can love your family without being treated like we're fourteen years old.

There are lots of ways in which I can be involved with the next generation, ways that tap into the gifts, wisdom, and love I have to offer while filling my capacity for cuteness, silliness, and messiness. Outlets for parental expression may come vocationally through career choices, or by volunteerism with programs that service and teach children and youth, or through friendship with those who have children. I remember reading of one single woman who so desired to be a mother that she moved to an impoverished community in order to work at an orphanage and have dozens of children.

Sometimes the desire for children may require a single person to avoid children for a while, to hurt and heal from the pain of disappointed dreams. Allowing God to meet us in our desire requires us to let go of the family we thought we would have in order to embrace the one he is already providing.

The fully realized version of this kind of church family is unfortunately not what many of us experience today. We may use Christianese to call each other brothers and sisters in Christ, but the truth is that many iterations of church community are far from being the kind of family one can rely on to help raise children, nurse the sick, or take care of retirees. Just because we as God's people haven't yet stepped up to his vision of family doesn't mean we can't move towards it now, but doing so will necessitate some reimagining of what's possible.

A change is required in order for all members of God's family to be cared for, utilized, and treated with dignity. Jesus and his apostles laid out a strong theological foundation to help us advocate for this kind of change and inclusivity. There is already a substantial amount of Christian energy devoted to the family in a modern context. What if we shifted some of that focus from trying to help everyone find a partner and raise children to making sure we're all included and behaving as the family of God?

So who in your life needs a daughter or a son? Who needs a brother or sister, uncle or aunt? Who needs a maternal or paternal voice in their life? What needs can you be meeting? Where can you use your gifts? With whom can you share your love? Who is your family? Who is the head of your household?

EXPERIENCING LONELINESS

> *...the depth of the pain of our loneliness is an
> indicator of the height of the union for
> which we were made.*[34]
> —John Ortberg

WHILE I'VE REALIZED that I don't need a spouse or children to be purposeful, successful, fulfilled, or happy, one thing has become clear: I will always need community.

God designed us for relationships. Times of solitude, even loneliness, can have a constructive impact on us, but God intentionally sets those who are lonely in families (Psalm 68:6) and hopes we will help each other up (Ecclesiastes 4:10). Jesus prayed that we would all be one (John 17:21). God intends for us to meet our mutual needs regardless of whether we marry.

But the reality many singles face is more difficult. While you may agree with Jesus's definition of family in theory, finding it is an entirely different matter. I don't think being single is a problem, but as research and likely your own experiences tells you, loneliness has become a chronic problem in our modern age.

Loneliness isn't a plight limited to the single person. Being single isn't the same as being lonely, nor is being coupled the same as being unlonely. Times of feeling invisible and isolated, of being disconnected, of not being heard, of yearning to be witnessed and recognized, are common to the human experience.

However loneliness and isolation may overlap with singleness in a way that can be profound and severe.

LONELINESS AS A HUMAN CONDITION

> fall
> in love
> with your solitude[35]
> — Rupi Kaur

Sometimes loneliness is something we can't avoid. The fact, however unjust, is that we will go through seasons of loss, rejection, transition, betrayal, and disconnection. There are occasions when we can feel totally unseen, thoroughly misunderstood, and long for more meaningful connection. This type of loneliness forces us to reckon with our humanness, our need, and our worthiness.

Something that can take the pressure off in these seasons, is to recognize how normal loneliness is. While it's painful, and hopefully eventually remedied, there may be value in learning to sit with this type of loneliness rather than rush to correct it, or at the very least not assume you're crazy or damaged for experiencing it. Loneliness can teach us a lot about how we're wired, about how we derive our sense of worth, and about our coping mechanisms.

It's a condition that transcends personality. While the introvert may be naturally more inclined to solitude and the extravert more inclined to social situations, we all want to be loved and known.

This loneliness is often parodied in film, likely because laughter is easier than tears. Consider the woman pouting over her ice cream or the man sulking over his beer. But in reality loneliness can produce a depth of emotional pain that no pint of ice cream or beer can remedy.

When we resist experiencing loneliness, we can do stupid things. We may choose distractions and devices that numb us and temporarily keep us from what we fear. But usually these things only drive us further into isolation. Many addictions and maladaptive behaviours find their roots in loneliness.

But the lessons of resilience and perseverance still apply. Loneliness can be endured. When greeted constructively, lonely times and the pain they bring can prime us for missional focus and creative expression. Many a great song has been composed, painting rendered, and handiwork constructed out of the burden of loneliness. If we let it, loneliness can catalyse risk and bravery. The part of us that is exhausted with it pushes us out of our comfort zone.

Whether we like it or not, loneliness is often the thing that draws us closer into relationship with the Holy Spirit. As Psalm 34:18 tells us, *"The Lord is close to the brokenhearted and saves those who are crushed in spirit."* God knows what it is to be lonely. As a creator-father, he knows the distance of a people who cannot grasp his heart or trust his direction. As one who was embodied among us, he knows the disloyalty of those who betrayed, disowned, and doubted him, those who couldn't even be bothered to wait up and pray for him.

He doesn't expect our lives to be free of pain, but he wants to be invited into it—to comfort, to heal, and to be with us. It is here that we begin to see our value. This is where we find our courage, our armour (Ephesians 6:10–18), and are equipped for good works (2 Timothy 3:17).

Facing my own loneliness has also involved a great deal of learning how to improve my relationship with myself. As I've become more aware of this, I realize how often people can neglect this very important relationship.

When I was providing individual counselling, my first stop with a client who was struggling with the common issues of self-image, worth, identity, or value was to introduce them to the idea of meta-processing: thinking about their thinking. I asked them to undertake a simple exercise designed to help them notice their self-talk—as in, what they said to themselves in their own heads throughout the day. Nearly every time I asked a client to spend the week noticing the sentences in their brain, they would return the next session astonished at just how mean their internal monologue had been. This would normally segue into me saying something along the lines of, "If you said those words to someone else out loud, you would be accused of bullying and harassment." The work then becomes less about stopping self-bullying behaviour and more about forging a new relationship by exploring a key question: "How can I be a better friend to me?"

It's possible that an uncomfortable but simple truth is lurking beneath the malcontent of your singleness: you don't like your own company very much. Or at least you don't know your own worth. Solitude can certainly give rise to unresolved darkness within us. This may very well require you to do some therapeutic work of your own in the company of a trusted counsellor, mentor, or spiritual leader. Some of the work may involve shifting your patterns to permit you to be the best and most fun version of yourself.

You'll probably find similar advice in dating books, or books about preparing for marriage, that if you want to attract a partner, you first must become attractive. There is some wisdom in this, because it's certainly a tall order to ask someone else to value in you what you don't value in yourself. But I think it's important for the single to know how beneficial it is to be an interesting person regardless of whether that ever attracts a mate or not. The question is, does it attract you? Do you like spending time with you? Have you found hobbies and activities that bring you joy and allow you to express your unique self?

We're often not taught how to be authentic, monitor our inner dialogue, be comfortable when alone, and enjoy our own company.

For lack of a better way of putting it, we need to learn how to date ourselves. In doing so, we'll learn that the life of a single is one of constant reframes. Tables can have just one chair, movie tickets can be purchased individually, and a life worth living is worth pursuing, period, regardless of who joins the journey. Taking responsibility for our own actions, direction, and relationships can move us further ahead in life than waiting for someone to romance us. Lacking this sense of identity is problematic for singles and couples alike, who may look to unhealthy ways of completing themselves.

Solitude was never meant to replace community, but it can be a lot more pleasant than you may have experienced. Being alone doesn't have to mean feeling lonely. Exploring my interests, discovering my preferences, figuring out my dislikes, getting creative about adapting to solo activities, challenging myself to expand my comfort zone, and embracing my personality quirks are all practices that have increased my confidence and made my life exponentially happier. It's not the same thing as having the company of others, but it has made difficult seasons much more enjoyable and much less scary.

LONELINESS AS A CHOICE

> The greatest hazard in life is to risk nothing.[36]
> —Leo Buscaglia

Oftentimes loneliness is of our own making. The irony is that the pain is actually the result of desperately trying to avoid other types of pain, be it rejection, loss, or the damage caused by the people we let get close.

In doing so, we make choices that isolate ourselves from others. We may choose not to be open or vulnerable. We stop letting people in. We may avoid the risk of rejection by not socializing. We may prefer to have our independence and preemptively exclude ourselves from company. Perhaps we hold onto bitterness and withhold forgiveness in relationships that have caused us pain because it makes us feel like we're in control. It's easy to feel justified in this, because people are messy, fallible, and annoying while the faux connection of our virtual worlds is compliant and submissive.

Loneliness may also be connected to jealousy. This can show up in many forms, but I'm thinking especially of the anxiety and sadness that can be caused by invitations to weddings, showers, or any event with happy couples and families, or the discomfort that can be associated with sitting through a church service on Mother's or Father's Day. Even when these feelings come from a place of deep legitimate pain, it's still envy—and it can be ugly. We may be so paralyzed by jealousy of someone else's life that being in community just hurts too much. Rather than be around another couple, announcement, or celebration, we wall ourselves off from the very community we need.

Life isn't fair and often causes us to feel robbed of joy. We feel jealous of the advantage we sense in others. Celebration is the key to overcoming this envy. Paul challenges us to *"rejoice with those who rejoice"* (Romans 12:15).

This requires us to stop thinking like Darwinists. The more we're influenced by a survival-of-the-fittest, dog-eat-dog, best-man-wins mentality, the harder it will be to celebrate with others.

As Jesus's followers, we must remind ourselves of a different truth: God loves and has a plan for all of us. We won't all get the same opportunities, but that doesn't decrease our value or purpose in God's sight. This divine approval doesn't come from anything we could earn; it comes from his indiscriminate grace. Recognizing that you don't deserve the accolades or experiences you feel you're owed will release the grip of jealousy in your life.

Another release can come from being thankful for threats. It's usually hardest to rejoice with someone who has something we wish we had, or is seeing more success in an area for which we seek acknowledgement. Pausing to thank God in these situations doesn't seem like a natural response, but it is powerful. By choosing to be thankful when we feel threatened, we actively place our identity in Christ rather than in our performance or possessions, reminding ourselves of God's sovereignty, timing, and resourcefulness. Once we release our identities from the constraints of our ability or insecurity, we're free to compliment others in their strengths and share in their joys.

Sometimes we wear our loneliness as a badge of honour, holding a grudge against God and proving to him that the reason we're miserable is because he hasn't provided for us romantically. We may even think that by maintaining this loneliness we are leaving room for a spouse, out of a fear that embracing the reality of our singleness and finding friends will mean that God won't answer our prayers for marriage.

Just as avoiding the bathroom scale won't keep you from being the weight you are, avoiding the parts of singleness that make it real for you won't make it any less real. This is a hard truth.

Navigating this type of loneliness can be a process, often a therapeutic one, that involves surrender, exposure, and healing. The truth is that there is a logic to this loneliness, and it requires courage for us to overcome it. Allowing people to get close enough to hurt you is brave. Investing in friendships that may change can be terrifying. Relying on other single friends who may move on to romance makes us fearful. And even if we're willing to cultivate a single life, we may fear that we'll grow to love it so much that romance will feel disruptive should it ever come along.

I once accepted a challenge to be committed enough to my single life that it would hurt to lose it. I remember Annie F. Downs and Andrea Lucado discussing this topic using a gardening analogy. Blooming where I'm planted means that my roots go deep. In the event of a transplant, some of the plants might get torn up.[37]

It's okay to know what I have to lose. It's okay to care about the things I might miss out on later. It's okay to know exactly what I'd be giving up if a relationship ever came along.

But hoping for romance someday doesn't need to doom my social life today. It's okay to invest fully in the present, to dive into friendships knowing that the future may have some loss associated with it. To guard against choosing loneliness out of fear, I must delight in the here and now.

YOU ARE NOT ALONE

> No man is an island entire of itself; every man is
> a piece of the continent, a part of the main…[38]
> —John Donne

You are not alone in being alone. The enemy would love all of us single people to believe the lie that we're on our own, isolated, the last of the remaining faithful, and therefore woefully lonely and impossibly misunderstood. The truth is that there are other singles out there, other friends, other Christians, other people with whom life can be shared. Many struggle with loneliness, longing, and self-management. This is true outside the church too. The more open I become about my struggles, the more I find other single people who are struggling with the same thing. And the more we share with each other, the more we are healed and helped by the simple truth that someone else gets it.

If the bad news of our world today is chronic loneliness, the good news for our generation can be found in relationship. I think if we could emphasize friendships more than romance, we would be astonished at the evangelistic power it holds.

Jesus said that others will know us as his disciples by our love for each other (John 13:35). The greatest evangelistic tool we have at our disposal is how we connect with other believers. This type of friendship is magnetic, this type of community therapeutic. It declares to those around us who seek meaning, friendship, and wholeness that there is an answer to the holes in their hearts, a place for them to belong, be seen, and be loved.

PRACTICING THE ART OF FRIENDSHIP

Find a group of people who challenge and inspire you; spend a lot of time with them, and it will change your life.[39]
—Amy Poehler

ONE STEP I think we the church could take towards addressing the burden of loneliness is to admit that, as a rule, we are not great at doing friendship. Some of this may be due to the isolationist nature of social media and our self-serve society. But a greater reason is that we've spent so much time focusing on romance as the means of satisfying all relational needs, that we've forgotten about the necessary art of friendship.

While there are lots of conferences, books, and sermons about how to get along in a spousal relationship, very little Christian energy is spent on teaching us how to do friendship beyond high school level. We may be able to find literature about making a marriage last, but there isn't much advice out there for people whose condiments have been in their lives longer than many of their friendships. In some cases, singles may actually have the relational advantage. They learn and can demand maturity from their relationships, or expose immaturity faster than those who are married. Couples, especially those who met at a young age, may be so focused on marriage and the obligations of family that they're distracted from or naïve to how deep platonic friendship can go and how much it can require of us.

It's easy for a single person to look over at the green grass of family and envy it for its built-in social network, but a recent conversation with a married colleague reminded me of the downside to that equation. She was feeling guilty about the limited number of connections she could maintain due to so much of her social energy being required by her family. In this way, the single may have more opportunity for community than those who are coupled.

Ostensibly a single can be friends with more people, hold multiple hobbies and interests simultaneously, and be responsive to friends in need without coordinating other people's schedules. Singles may have the head and heart space to care about many people and make connections without worrying about whether their partner will get along with them or feel jealous. While a coupled person devotes much of their relational energy to one individual, the single may direct love and relational energy to multiple outposts.

One woman told me that she doesn't even like the word single because she is never so connected to the rest of humanity as when she is single. She described being single as being connected at all three hundred sixty degrees rather than just one hundred eighty.

It may take some creativity, and some out-of-the-box thinking, but there are deep and meaningful human connections available to singles.

The idea of relationship is that life is experienced together. Perhaps the biggest answer to breaking out of a lonely spiral or finding relationship is just to get together with other people, to be interested in their lives and take our minds off ourselves. In our isolation as singles, it's easy to conclude that our lives are all about our dreams when in reality God may have positioned us to be part of making someone else's dream come true, or to get so close to another person that their dream becomes our dream.

Servant-heartedness culminates in shared vision. The deeper I involve myself in community, the more I see victories and losses as collective. By putting others first and investing in their stories, suddenly their wins become our wins, their sorrows our burdens. This is how we extend our sense of family and widen our relationship circle.

I don't think there is any entry point into such a deep friendship that isn't awkward. Nor do I think success can be measured by the speed at which this awkwardness subsides. If you're single long enough, it's going to force you to learn how to make friends, and you may have to attempt to do so with a lot of people who are worse at it than you. There will always be time, energy, trial, and error involved in finding those friendships.

As a rule, coupled relationships come with twice the access to human contact through a doubling of family, work, and volunteer contexts. When kids are in the mix, there are even more opportunities through schools, neighbourhood events, and various sports and activities, not to mention the built-in small talk about diapers, daycares, and little leagues.

While singles have more freedom and flexibility, our social worlds don't adhere to the same norms. We may not bond over being single the same way others bond over being married or being parents, and it can be harder to find things we have in common. This is especially true if our only chances to be together are in a quasi-competitive setting with other singles vying for limited romantic attention. Even when we do bond over singleness, a person's relationship status isn't static. Our friendships shift, change, or are lost altogether when our single friends transition into relationships. Also, it's likely that singles don't just want to find other singles to hang out with, but the options for connection outside of a singles group are often limited to parents, couples, and events we get fewer invitations to as the contents shift to family matters.

Friendship can be amazing, but finding it can be hard work—especially when you don't have the rose-tinted, flaw-overlooking glasses that the infatuation of romance provides. You may have to go to a church for a long time, try out more than one small group, and attend more than one uncomfortable outing reserved for young people, singles, career-minded, divorced, or widowed adults. You'll likely have to endure awkward side hugs and sweaty handshakes, fumble through disjointed conversations, and feign amusement at many humourless jokes. You may need to take a crafting class, join a sports team or running club, or take part in a band or choir. You may need to volunteer, join a board, or take up part-time work. It might mean getting rejected multiple times, saying hello to a stranger, or boldly inviting someone with whom you've engaged in some small talk to take it to the next level. You may need to plan events to which you can invite others and have the resilience to withstand being stood-up and the confidence to not feel as if you're bribing people to spend time with you. It may feel inauthentic, intrusive, and even manipulative to inject yourself into another person's social world.

Some of these efforts will eventually transform into the friendships you've been seeking. Some will become the anecdotes you tell the next time you're stuck for a topic of conversation. Just remember that every significant relationship you've ever had started out as a conversation with a stranger.

And yes, most of this effort sounds similar to the effort many single people already put into dating culture. But I wonder, how different might the outcomes be without the romantic imperative?

Most of this friendship advice can apply to those in couples too, but many will first have to overcome the barrier of assuming that all their social needs should be met through their partner. Another casualty of our cultural obsession with romance is that so many people in couples actually feel quite lonely but are afraid that it means they're failing at love.

In many ways, making friends hasn't evolved much since childhood. Sometimes it really is as simple as picking a kid on the playground and asking them to be your friend.

When life doesn't naturally present bonding opportunities, there are three practices guaranteed to deepen our connectedness as humans: being vulnerable, serving others, and submitting to accountability.

VULNERABILITY

> Until we can receive with an open heart, we are never really giving with an open heart. When we attach judgment to receiving help, we knowingly or unknowingly attach judgment to giving help.[40]
> —Brené Brown

Years ago, I babysat a boy who was struggling to learn his manners. As the second of five children myself (a.k.a. Mom #3), I had become adept at ensuring that pleases, thank-yous, and apologies were nonoptional and was eager to implement my methods on a rather insolent three-year-old.

After lunch one day, he asked for an additional snack, to which I requested that he say please. His refusal to do so led to a lengthy afternoon of delicate choreography wherein he would motion towards the bunch of grapes, I would pleasantly tell him, "Yes, you may absolutely have some grapes, just say please," and he would duck coyly around a corner. After forty-five long minutes, he sulked into the kitchen, dropped his head in surrender, and whispered in a quaint childish accent, "Peeze." For which I cheered and provided many grapes.

There may be better examples than the manners of toddlers to demonstrate this, but *please* is more than a word. It's more than a social grace or nicety. Please is an attitude, the recognition of our need for others. It is, in essence, a way of saying "Help."

For most of us, our first real approach to God could be distilled into that same word. And while God doesn't dangle a carrot, or grapes, in front of us until we use the magic words, he does place some limits on himself and his intervention until we ask for it, not because he demands politeness or formality but out of respect for our free will.

Until we're willing to surrender to God and acknowledge our need of him, we simply aren't ready for the magnitude of grace and blessing he is waiting for us to accept. We have a choice. We can either stubbornly wander around grumbling and pointing at all we think we want out of life while pretending we don't need him, or we can humble ourselves before him and allow him to provide.

Scripture consistently draws a link between acknowledging our need and that need being met. Provision isn't tied to our worthiness but our helplessness (James 4:6).

In his most famous sermon, Jesus poetically states what are known as the beatitudes: you are blessed when you are poor in spirit, mourning, meek, hungry, thirsty, and persecuted—in other words, you are blessed when you need (Matthew 5:3–11). Need is a blessing because in it God meets you with provision.

Of course, asking for God's help is only the first step. More often than not, he provides that help through people, and asking for and receiving help from others requires us to surrender our pride.

For a long time, I thought the key to single success was to be fully independent. When it came to adult responsibilities, I learned to sort tasks into one of three categories: things I do, things I pay people to do, and things I leave undone. I spent many years trying unsuccessfully to be a jack of all trades before realizing there was a fourth category I had omitted: things I ask for help with. I don't know that there was a day of conscious decision to stop asking for help; rather, I think I unlearned the skill through years of living on my own, experiencing rejection and embarrassment, and maybe even feeling like a burden.

I do, however, remember the day when I decided to start asking for help again.

I had been sick for an extended period of time and running out of the supplies I usually keep on hand just in case: ginger ale, crackers, soup, tissues, cough remedies, tea, etc. While lying in bed with terrible aches in my stomach and head, fantasizing about my mommy flying into town to take care of me, a friend texted to check in. Was there anything they could do?

My pride got in the way.

"No, thank you," I watched myself text in response to this offer of help. "I think I'll be okay."

What was that? It was beyond a white lie. I desperately needed the help and it had presented itself so conveniently. Why had I rejected it? It wasn't even the only offer I received that day. Other friends and co-workers had sent their respective versions of "Let me know if there's anything I can bring you." I had stupidly, politely, and pridefully declined those too.

What was it about me that wanted not to need someone?

Mercifully, this particular friend double-checked: "Are you sure? It's not a big deal!"

I had a shot at a redo and knew I had to be more honest. "Actually, yeah, some soup and crackers and ginger ale would be amazing. I'm kind of out of everything."

Even after agreeing to her popping by with these supplies, I wanted to be less needy. Had I not been dealing with some serious vertigo, I would have done a mad scramble to remove the evidence of illness from my surroundings. I later realized this was more a gift in the lesson of humility than it was a gift of chicken soup. This was about being the raw, authentic, pyjama'd, snot-nosed version of me, the one who actually doesn't have a sparkling clean home when she's been sick for a week—the me who had to reckon with the possibility of inconveniencing someone.

Nobody likes to be vulnerable, but everybody wants to feel useful. When I'm the one who hears about a sick friend or learns of someone who's grieving or requires help, I'm overjoyed at the prospect of being useful and genuinely mean it when I offer to help. On those few occasions when my offers of meals, errand runs, hospital visits, or hugs are accepted, I am delighted to be of service.

But when I'm offered help, it's a different story.

I can think of many other examples from recent years when I had to swallow my pride and let someone do something for me, and often in much more intimate ways. I'm slowly getting better at dropping the mask of independence long enough to ask for assistance with my car, moving furniture around, getting rides to the airport, or accepting help for an abundance of other tasks I would typically try to deal with alone.

To protect myself from the ache that can accompany singleness, I had walled off the part of me that needed. Opening her up was, and continues to be, both beautiful and painful.

Admittedly, letting your guard down long enough to let someone do something for you can open the window to grief and fear. You may ask, "If I rely on this help now, what will I do if it's not there later?" Accepting help may poke holes in the grudge you might be holding against God for not meeting your needs in other ways. Perhaps God has provided for you in many ways and through many people, but you were blind to the support because it didn't come in the format you wanted. I'm still learning that it was never in God's design for me to not need the help of others, regardless of whether that help ever shows up in the form of a romantic partner.

This is my new interpretation of the often-weaponized verse: *"It is not good for the man to be alone"* (Genesis 2:18).

Jesus showed us in both large and small ways the power of being vulnerable. God incarnate forfeited the luxuries of position by choosing a human birth and sacrificial death that involved exposure to the least of humanity. His life on earth served as the ultimate expression of laying down the independence of power for the sake of becoming relational and accessible, and maybe inconvenient. It doesn't get much more needy than showing up as an infant in a barn!

But he also demonstrated simple ways of leading from vulnerability. Though himself the Messiah, Jesus allowed John the Baptist to baptize him (Matthew 3:13–17). He taught us to turn the other cheek (Matthew 5:39) and love our enemies (Matthew 5:44), and assured us that the least in the kingdom are actually the greatest (Luke 9:48). His nomadic ministry meant that he regularly dropped in and sought accommodations with people on short notice, modelling an interdependency that I find uncomfortable. He taught the disciples to receive help both when he served them by washing their feet (John 13:1–17) and when he permitted a woman to bathe his feet with her tears and dry them with her hair (Luke 7:36–38). Can you imagine letting someone do that for you?

In teaching and in practice, Jesus demonstrated that the things of God are revealed to those who are helpable—those who ask, seek, and knock... not those who answer, ignore, and have all the keys.

When he encountered the woman at the well, though he was fully aware of her past and her ultimate need, he initiated conversation by asking, *"Will you give me a drink?"* (John 4:7) He led from his own thirst, from their common humanity rather than any sense of uncommon divinity. Before moving into ministry mode, he allowed himself to need and allowed her to meet that need.

As I've become more gracious in accepting help, I've realized that to refuse or preclude it is actually a huge act of selfishness. Far from alleviating others of a burden, it deprives them of the joy of generosity and usefulness.

Accepting help is the way you give people around you permission to ask for and offer help themselves. Admitting that you need help is the way you stay connected to your humanity. It floats the test balloon out into the crowd to indicate that it's okay to need. It exposes our gaps long enough for others to see where and how they might step in.

This flies in the face of the independence movement, which traps us into thinking that it's desirable not to need. As long as we remain in our myth of independence and self-expertise, we will continue to create walls between us and others.

True vulnerability will extend beyond giving and receiving favours. Vulnerability moves us into a space of confession, redemption, mutual edification, and healing. This isn't to say that our entire lives need be an open book to everyone in our circle. Rather, there will be people whom we bring close enough that they truly see us.

Regardless of how I break it down, I can't do my life alone. I've gotten much better at asking for help, and offering it, and I can link the deepening of all my significant friendships to a moment when I either expressed need or accepted generosity.

As a single, I still sometimes think more strategically than relationally, and weigh the costs and balances of favours, but I'm slowly beginning to accept that even if all the requests settle out on my score sheet, I will still be in no less need of grace.

SERVICE

> Humility is not thinking less of yourself, it's thinking of yourself less.[41]
> —Rick Warren

Of course, receiving help is only one part of the relational equation. Vulnerability finds its counterbalance in service.

When the disciples asked Jesus to teach them how to pray, he answered with what we have come to know as the Lord's prayer. This prayer is consistently stated from a collective: "Our Father" instead of "my Father," "Give us today our daily bread" instead of "Give me today my daily bread," and so on (Matthew 6:9–13). Even in prayer, Jesus indicated that approaching God and receiving a response happens in a communal context. The petition is not "Give me what I need in order to do my life alone" but "Give us collectively what we need." The pieces of God's provision for you may require some assembly, as they may be spread across a group of people. This means that some of what we need may only be available when we gather together and exercise transparency and generosity.

God didn't design us as to be independent. This is why Jesus modelled the life of a servant. It's about more than volunteerism, which can be reward-motivated and often allows us to function in our comfort zone, sitting on the edge of community with a defined task that keeps us safe. It's also about more than an annual work bee organized by local nonprofits, or a quarterly missions trip to build a house in an impoverished region. Though those are good things.

Servanthood is about being attentive to and meeting needs for others regardless of position, acknowledgement, advancement, or sometimes even skill. It's about having an attitude that asks, "How can I help?" Whether it's leveraging your greatest ability entirely for another's benefit or performing a task completely detached from your skillset simply to meet a need, servanthood gets you out of your head, world, and problems and invests your energy, resources, and prayers into the story of another. Service flows from holding a perspective that the wealth, gifts, lessons, and strengths you've received aren't intended for you alone.

If there are areas in life where you feel like you aren't being provided for, perhaps that provision lies in the storehouse of another person. If there are issues in your life where you feel like you have more than enough, perhaps the extra is intended to be shared with someone else. The way of God is interdependency amongst his people.

A simple expression of this, especially in the context of singlehood, can be seen through small acts of kindness. Think of all the tasks, chores, and responsibilities that go into adulting. The cooking, the cleaning, the maintenance of the home or yard or car, the accounting, the shopping, the travel arranging, the party planning, the remembering to buy gifts and send cards... the list could go on. When you're in a couple, these tasks are somehow divided, even if in an unbalanced or dysfunctional way. Where there are two, there is usually some division of labour or at least shared brainstorming and troubleshooting on how to mitigate gaps. But as a single, all these tasks become the responsibility of one. And just because we have to do it all doesn't mean we like, have time for, or are competent at everything in our home management portfolios.

In a culture that assumes coupledom will eventually happen, these issues are often put off and thought of as deficiencies to be mitigated by a future partner rather than needs to be met in community.

This seems to be even more pronounced when traditional gender norms are presumed. For example, a single woman is encouraged to find a man who is handy. A man seeks to find a woman who can cook. In the meantime, both are expected to clumsily suffer through mac n' cheese and lopsided end tables until the answer comes along.

These can be overwhelming logistics for the single person. Our laundry shelves, pantry, and dish cabinets aren't stocked through bridal showers but years of practical birthday gifts, hand-me-downs and thrift store bargains. Sometimes YouTube is the only repairman we can afford. I can recall times when I've legitimately melted down over not being able to unscrew a lid from a jar, yank a cable from a wall, ignite a pilot light, or successfully deal with rodents and giant bugs. I distinctly remember having to ask my landlord to drive me to a dental appointment that required sedation because I literally had no one else to call.

There is some life hackery involved in adapting to the day-to-day. I now understand why my single grandmother always had the TV on in the background; I too can get restless without the company of other voices. I may need to go to message boards and podcasts to share in entertainment and hobbies with others. I use stools and tongs to reach things on the top shelf, and I have various ergonomic and athletic devices for working the knots out of my back. I have to be mindful of wearing clothing and jewellery that I can self-zip, clasp, tie, and buckle. And none of this is what I pictured what being an independent woman would mean.

I don't mean to imply that all these needs are automatically met in marriage. Rather, I'm emphasizing the damage that can be done when we expect that they ought to be.

The difficulty of this is compounded for single people when the same deficiencies in a couple scenario are automatically attended to by the church. For example, I can recall an instance when a young married man without kids was home alone for a week as his wife was travelling out of town. The meal prep team at church whipped into action to make sympathy food for him in order to ease the burden of his week "as a bachelor." I know of car care ministries that are dispatched to support recent divorcees whose husbands are no longer around to manage the auto affairs.

These are actually beautiful demonstrations of community and I'm grateful they exist. But it would be amazing to see similar courtesies consistently extended to the never-married. Furthermore, it would be amazing to see this type of need-meeting occur organically through relationships, not only programmed through church offices.

The challenge of living in a culture of immediacy and individualism is that we forget we have skills, talents, and resources that other people might need. I am by no means letting singles off the hook of service. Most people are likely suffering a bit from ill-attention, since we each have needs that could be met within community. We all have gifts to offer that are likely tarnishing from underuse. My guess is that many of us are also guilty of offering to pray about these issues without stepping up to actually be part of the answer.

Regardless of gender or skill, simple gestures can go a long way to relieve the burden of oneness. Offering to cook, repair, transport, lift, or clean something, to be the emergency contact person, or the airport shuttle driver, or the truck lender, or a myriad of other service offerings are all significant ways of recognizing the needs of singles and of demonstrating love. And they may be much more effective at doing so than the incessant matchmaking and unsolicited dating advice.

This information can also be used as vocabulary to both offer and recruit support, or at the very least to negotiate trades amongst your single friends. This can be messy and often doesn't seem equitable. Needs and service will not always have a direct or seemingly comparable quality. You might have a need in the area of emotional support but can give in the area of finances. Someone may give in the area of wisdom and knowledge but be given to with hospitality. You may sometimes feel indebted and other times feel owed. It's not about balancing a roster or ticking boxes, it's about bringing our all to relationships.

Regardless of your relationship status, the challenge to all of us is twofold: we must learn to become more servant-hearted in offering help to others, and to become more vulnerable in asking for and being willing to receive help from others.

ACCOUNTABILITY

I'm never quite so aware of my driving habits as when I'm taxiing other people's children around. While I would hardly characterize my solo driving as reckless, the chauffeuring of another person's precious cargo induces an acute sensitivity that perceives all stops as too short, all corners too sharp, and all speeds too fast. Similarly, a backseat of little people makes me more cognizant of my attitude behind the wheel. There's nothing like the monkey-see-monkey-do perspective of a toddler to ensure I bite my tongue when another car cuts me off.

The knowledge of being entrusted with another's life, in addition to the possibility of all the trip's details being relayed back to the first person to offer a chocolate milk bribe, is an immense amount of accountability to fit inside a hatchback.

Many people have expressed to me that one of their fears in being single for a long time is that they'll grow selfish or pick up weird habits. While requiring accountability isn't unique to the single experience, the challenge is that the accountability that guards against those behaviours requires a more intentional opt-in than casually waking up next to a spouse who can point out your snoring and dirty socks.

There's a lot of power held in the presence or absence of others. A community of witnesses can be a magnifier to expose our weaknesses, reveal our defaults, and offer opportunities to tweak our behaviour to address blemishes that are difficult to see in the mirror. Conversely, frequent seclusion can result in progressive laziness, decay, and desensitization to the role our habits play in our lives. Eventually vulnerability and service will lead us into spaces that demand more of us relationally. Sometimes we opt for loneliness because we just don't like the accountability that comes with being well-known.

My guess is that most of us know we need accountability, but the disruption and discomfort it can cause makes it a convenient topic to ignore. Online shopping, self-checkouts, and AI-informed environments feed us the lie that we can do life on our own. All the while, social media deceives us into thinking we're not alone. By selectively exposing only the internet-friendly version of truth to people held at an arm's length, we confuse publicity for transparency.

Likewise, in a culture obsessed with self-improvement, it's easy to adopt leadership jargon in place of authentic communication. By shaping a generation of leaders, we can forget that Christ first called us to be followers. We may mentally position ourselves outside, or even arrogantly above, the realm of legitimate feedback.

There is prudence in ensuring that our stories are treated with respect and care, but it's important to have people in our lives who we let into those non-edited places. The scriptures describe this as confession: *"Therefore confess your sins to each other and pray for each other so that you may be healed"* (James 5:16).

There is value in the simple act of disclosing our behaviour, such as in the confessional, during prayer time at church, at an AA meeting, in an online forum, or possibly through some type of therapy. That said, I believe that true accountability takes confession further than a quasi-anonymous disclosure. Accountability requires confession, consent, and community.

Confession is about sharing information about the parts of ourselves we would prefer to keep hidden.

Consent is about doing this voluntarily while giving permission for those to whom we confess to speak into the situation.

Community is about this happening in a relational context with people whose opinions count, whose lives are potentially impacted, and whose presence will continue beyond the disclosure.

The reason confession is healing isn't just that we get something off our chests. It's about more than having our disclosure witnessed by a second party. In confession we experience the power of community to show us compassion and lend us strength in knowing we are no longer doing life alone. Community bolsters us for future resistance to temptation too. I'm far less likely to engage in a behaviour that runs counter to my desires for my life when I know that the people who love me and understand my values are watching for signs of health and freedom and may even check in on me.

Of course, this only goes as far as I allow it to go. Accountability is nothing without consent. Someone can drag a story out of me, but I'll attach minimal significance to their advice if I'm not ready to hear it. When we force accountability on an unwilling party, at some point it just becomes a breach of boundaries.

When someone is close enough to us that their opinion matters, around us enough that they can observe our behaviours, trusted enough to know both our story and the values we're trying to live up to, and has our permission to enter our personal space and call us out, that is accountability. In this context, we find the resources to defend ourselves against selfishness, loneliness, impurity, and other ills, whether we remain single or not.

While we all experience seasons of loneliness, and can even benefit from deliberate spells of solitude, we were intended for community. It's much easier to justify not responding to community than it is to be humble and patient as we try to find it. But too much time in the proverbial car alone results in sloppy driving that can lead to dangerous collisions down the road. Signs that I am starting to sidestep accountability in my life include:

- when I find myself avoiding certain relationships for fear of the feedback I'll be given on a particular topic,
- if it has been a while since I ventured outside of my disclosure comfort zone,
- if I can't remember the last time somebody told me, "no" and it counted.

I'm not sure what your signals are, but when they show up it can be a good time to ask God to reveal the authentic sources of community he has made available. You can choose the company and service of others over the temptation toward self-centeredness and personal preference and embrace encounters that threaten the ego. If all else fails, offer to babysit!

HONOURING MARRIAGE

When I was a young girl and had trouble sleeping, my dad taught me to pray for those in my life who weren't Christians. His rationale was simple. If by chance my restlessness was being caused by some spiritual attack, such prayers would put an end to that agenda quickly. And if it wasn't, I'd at least be putting my sleeplessness to good use.

A similar thought occurred to me during a particular season of relationship envy. As soon as I wanted to revert into a state of self-pity and ask God to provide a partner for me, I was convicted instead to use the moment to pray God's will for all the marriages and couples I could think of.

Whether I ever get married, whether I actively pursue marriage, I can always honour that institution. One way to do so is to focus on valuing existing marriages. Value can be shown in how we speak and think about, pray for, and interact with those who are married. In fact, a great way to reduce stigma, increase mutual understanding, and break down barriers to community is for singles and marrieds to do life alongside each other.

As a single, I enjoy spending time with my married friends and relatives, as well as with their kids. I recognize that some of these conversations will involve coupley things and parenting topics. That's okay. That's what's going on in the lives of the people I love. I think marrieds benefit from the perspective of the singles around them too. We can add value, insight, conversation, and entertainment to our married friends through sharing what's going on our personal lives, work lives, and yes, maybe even dating lives.

What frustrates me is how many times I see singles excluded from social events, as if we're in an episode of a costume drama and the host needs to balance a dinner table. I'm not sure why one is such an uncomfortable number. I can't believe how often singles are excluded from certain events or treated awkwardly. More than once, me and my single siblings have been invited to an event passively, through a relative or group invite, when all the couples we know receive personal invitations. It takes effort not to be offended that our presence isn't worth the postage or an extra email.

Singles can come too! Many of us want to come. We have lives and sometimes interesting things going on in them. There is more to life and adulthood than romance and parenting. We can talk about our work, friends, families, current events, books, movies, music, theology, politics, and even the weather. We can engage in and attend sporting matches, hikes, games, concerts, and recitals. Not every point of bonding needs to be about the parts of family we don't have in common.

But navigating relationships with couples can have its own challenges and require energy and boundaries. Attraction isn't static, and neither is relational security. While cross-gender, cross-couple friendship can be amazing and beneficial, it isn't without potential complications which are made worse by assuming that no harm will ever follow because we're all "just friends." Other times, it's assumed that a single person is so starved for romance that they'll break up another person's relationship to get it.

The latter is a stigma that is particularly fatiguing and painful. Freeing ourselves to value singleness and not place so much emphasis on finding a partner can alleviate some of the mythology among friends and family that every person without a ring must be a sexual threat.

But knowing this dynamic exists requires a balancing act of not vilifying singles while also establishing healthy boundaries.

A helpful concept from my counsellor training is the idea that my client isn't actually either of the people in the relationship but the relationship itself. My client is the marriage. While this doesn't apply exactly in a social context, the idea has been useful to my relationships with couples. When I'm friends with someone who is married, even if I relate more to one half of the couple than the other, I do my best to consider the couple "one" and to be friends with "them," at least on some level. While I will happily keep confidences for my girlfriends, it's always done with an aim to support honesty and transparency in their relationship, not to be a party to division.

That rule applies even more so to the husband in the relationship. I try to avoid most private or offline conversations and always try to speak of the partner with respect. This isn't easy, and sometimes it's even annoying, as it can mean including people I get along with less for the sake of respecting a relationship.

For the same reason, when I work or volunteer with a man, I do my very best to befriend his wife or girlfriend early on. I try to apply these rules to social media interactions as well. And anytime something shifts in my own heart or mind regarding the "just friends" issue, I'm quick to be open with someone who can hold me accountable for my behaviour and boundaries. I can't control how someone else's husband chooses to interact with me, nor can I take ownership for a lack of trust in someone else's relationship or dictate how my intentions are interpreted, but I can be transparent and vigilant about how I interact with him. I can be aware of physical contact, joking, or anything that would show me to be closer or more intimate with him than his partner might be.

This mindset of honouring marriage can extend to other behaviours too, such as being mindful of how relationships are depicted in the entertainment I consume, how I respond when relationships end, or simply how I discuss the topic of marriage. It's far too easy to pivot from looking for the good in singleness and the reality in marriage to hunting for the problems in marriage to make myself feel better about the hard parts of being single. One of the ways I try to honour marriage is simply by holding a desire for it in tension with living a full single life.

A single person can honour marriage in dating too. In a world of increasing complexity around marriage and divorce, the single has much to navigate. This is challenging when so many in the dating pool have a marriage or more in their history, or when good people seeking relational wholeness may pursue romance before they've processed their last relationship. It's complicated further by the fact that so many people choose not to marry these days, so that the casual glance at the left ring finger isn't the green light it used to be. No wonder Paul said that it was better to be single! No wonder the disciples asked Jesus whether it was easier to not get married!

Being close enough to God, open to his word, and secure in our singleness are great steps to take before navigating such challenging terrain.

Despite these efforts on my part, I have still been perceived as a romantic threat, and I personally know many other singles who have felt a similar sneer of derision from members of a couple who got the wrong idea. I think this is more about other people than it is about us, but it's still difficult and hurtful. I wish the world wouldn't conflate a seeking single with a prowling animal. There's not much I can do about that but remain accountable and open before God, dancing the tension between not forfeiting my freedom on account of another's insecurity or sin and yet being willing to sacrifice my preferences out of love for others.

Whether I ever get married, I want to be someone who honours marriage. The more I pursue true relationships, deep community, and the connectedness of extended family, the more this honour is required.

KINDRED SPIRITS

> In the sweetness of friendship let there be laughter, and sharing of pleasures. For in the dew of little things the heart finds its morning and is refreshed.[42]
> —Kahlil Gibran

There are different seasons and stages of friendship. There may be contrasts in how this plays out as we age, though, and we will also feel varying degrees of compatibility, closeness, and trust with different people.

Some friends we may see daily or weekly while others we catch up with only when they're in town. Some we may outgrow and others may be more acquaintances with whom we connect irregularly. Some friends are older and provide sage advice while others are younger and help keep us young while exercising our older sibling muscles. Others still are our peers. There are friends who are so similar to us that it's scary and others who couldn't be more different yet draw something out of us that is important. Some friends are more like family. Some family members are our closest friends. Some friendships allow us to be childlike, others to vent creative energy, and others draw out our seriousness and depth.

When we're privileged enough to have friendship, we practice intimacy and selflessness as well as communal rejoicing and mourning.

The new command Jesus gave is for us to love one another as he loves us (John 13:34). The act of love is so encompassing that it summarizes every commandment that preceded it and includes all behaviour required to thrive in a godly life. The command shows that the experience of love, of knowing and being known, isn't reserved for the few or the married. In fact, God promises his presence wherever two or three are gathered (Matthew 18:20).

God literally lives in relationship.

On the other side of the daunting process of seeking friendships are the sometimes rare and beautiful moments when we uncover a bonafide confidante, an in-case-of-emergency person, or a "kindred spirit."[43] These are the people who laugh with us, cry with us, can predict our responses, push our buttons, and generally delight in who we are. And the feeling is mutual.

I haven't always had these kinds of friendships in my life, but the seasons when I have are among the sweetest I've known. The weightiness of my singleness has always been eased in their presence—spiritually, emotionally, and logistically.

While I longed for it, I also used to be scared of friendship like this, as I could only imagine that degree of closeness happening for me in the context of romance.

I now fight for friendship in a way I didn't before, both in terms of its validity and its quality. I don't protect myself from being interdependent with friends out of a fear of scaring away potential romantic suitors, though I've been given that advice more than once. I also no longer operate out of fear that the friendship will change if one of us gets married. At the same time, I've become more discerning about the company I keep and generally try to avoid people or social settings that make me feel sad or left out due to my singleness.

Such intimacy teaches me to be intentionally changed by the people in my life and not to reserve such transformation for a potential marriage. I have built family-style rituals around holidays, meals, and coffee dates with the people closest to me. I ensure that the physical affection of hugs and snuggles is routine for those in my inner circle. I have in-jokes, songs, and specific TV shows, movies, foods and beverages that I reserve for particular company. I have found people to travel, be entertained, and create memories with.

And yes, all of this can and probably will change, and I'm sure some of those changes will carry hurt, but the experience of being known is worth it to me. I regularly give thanks to God for bringing me these friendships and trust that in his love and abundance he will continue his work in my life so that my fear doesn't hold me in scarcity. This allows me to jump into relationships—both feet, heart abandoned, willing to take on the joy and the pain of sharing life with other people.

I don't share about this because I think it's common, but for you to know that it is possible. I actually think this kind of friendship is rare. I know I felt like I discovered gold when I found it.

It's even hard to find examples of this in stories, particularly those portrayed in modern entertainment that seems to only know how to dramatize sexual attraction.

But it's worth pursuing, maybe even more so than romance. Whether it looks like the innocence of Anne and Diana of Green Gables, the adventures of Baker Street's Sherlock Holmes and Dr. Watson, the loyalty of Israel's David and Jonathan, or something else entirely, we understand more of God's love and his intention for humanity when our souls find connection with another.

PART FOUR

EMBRACE A NEW
Reality

LOVING WHAT IS

Contentment is not the fulfillment of what you want, but the realization of how much you already have.
—Unknown

I REMEMBER ONE hard day very near the end of my 4 year tenure as both a full-time employee and full-time grad student during which twelve-to-sixteen hour days were the norm. After this particular day of frustrating meetings, with some paperwork and housework still looming, I walked in my door exhausted at 9:00 p.m. I was hungry, grumpy, tired, and more than a little annoyed to greet an empty, neglected home that was somehow more akin to a toxic waste dump than a professional woman's apartment.

I kicked off my shoes into the growing pile of footwear, dumped the various bags from my arms into the fire-hazardous accumulation of end-of-day clutter, and opened the door of the science experiment formerly known as my refrigerator. Then, for thirty whole seconds, I daydreamed about a strong, handsome man welcoming me home with dinner, giving me a foot rub and an opportunity to vent about my day.

Before I could complete the fantasy, though, my rational mind jerked me back to reality: "No, if you came home to a husband, some of this mess would be his and you'd feel guilty about yours. Most likely you'd have to sort out dinner for two people and you'd have to show compassion you don't have, to hear about someone else's day too. You don't want a husband. You want a butler!"

I cite this moment often in encouraging other singles to stop romanticizing marriage. It's never wise to make comparisons (2 Corinthians 10:12), but my experience is that most people who struggle to realize the joy of singleness view it in the unrealistic shadow of glamourized coupledom. We have an unfortunate habit of comparing the worst parts of singleness to the best parts of being in a couple, yet rarely consider the other half of that equation. We seldom acknowledge how much pressure this puts on a romantic relationship to meet needs it wasn't designed to meet, or the sense of failure or incompletion couples can feel on the other side of "I do."

By making romance everything, we don't give permission for marriage to feel challenging or disappointing, and we don't give ourselves permission to see some of its limitations and even flaws.

Early on in the days of self-isolation and social distancing that accompanied the 2020 lockdowns in my part of the pandemic world, I remember chatting with one of my married friends on the phone.

"I don't think I've seen another human physically in fourteen days," I bemoaned.

Her prompt reply both humbled and humoured me. "I don't think I've been *alone* in fourteen days!"

It's unbalanced to scrutinize the burdens of singleness while observing the benefits of romance through a biased filter. Both lives carry their joys and burdens, their freedoms and limitations.

One reason it can be so hard to embrace singleness is that the benefits of being single can sound like selfishness to the married ear. This might be because a secular perspective of single independence can lean towards a self-centred attitude, or it could be that within Christianity marriage and family are connected to such deeply held values that the benefits of singlehood can be cast as superficial.

Whatever the reason, the virtues of singleness may need to be redeemed in some contexts. Not every encounter has to be challenged as an opportunity for re-education, but I've gotten more confident and vigilant about standing up for all that my singleness has to offer me.

I recall a conversation with a friend of mine who had small children. We were casually chatting when she asked about what I had done over the weekend. I had barely begun—"Well, on Saturday I slept i..."—when she immediately interjected to recount the sorrowful tale of how her husband, children, and pets had all prevented her from sleeping in for over a decade. This wasn't the first time I had been on the receiving end of such remarks. When I was younger, I took similar interactions as personal chastisements and either received some form of shame for not being more mature or wallowed in the fact that I didn't have a similar story about having a family to get up and make pancakes for. That version of me would never have dreamt about challenging a sleep-deprived mother to a competition over who had suffered most.

But I had since decided that it's actually an amazing privilege and benefit of singleness to have such a tremendous amount of control over how much I sleep. I can sleep in on weekends. I can go to bed early when I feel like it and stay up late when I don't. Outside of work obligations, I can nap to compensate for poor sleep or sit around being lazy and grumpy when I'm tired without it impacting anyone but me. All the while, I still carry on as an adult, grow in my career, serve my community, and do a thousand other responsible grown-up things.

So this time I felt equipped to respond correctively: "You know, I would love to have a husband in my bed and a baby in my arms to wake me up on the weekends, but those are some of your blessings. One of mine is that I got to stay in bed until noon."

To survive a coupled world as a single requires us to stop living as if we're in a couple. I don't think non-singles are malicious, but they may just be ignorant or unintentionally negligent when it comes to these matters. Because most people default to thinking about living in pairs, it can be work to consider the single life. And this work and extra thinking it takes to consider the requirements and benefits for single people in a couple-centric society can often lead to blaming singles for being selfish. I don't think there is a one-size-fits-all response to the stigma and marginalization this can cause, but I think it's worth trying to address in some fashion.

Once at a Christian conference, I was assigned to share a hotel room and bed with a teenaged girl I had never met in order to save the organizers the money of booking a separate room. The couples didn't have to share rooms with strangers, of course. This experience is all too common. Singles often regale me with stories about it being assumed they will sleep on the couch or the floor while couples get the guest rooms at family functions. Others share of being seated at the children's table at events. One friend commented that any time he dines alone in a restaurant he is assigned to sit near the kitchen or bathrooms or is given a barstool instead of a table. Some are forced to work on holidays because those with less seniority "have families."

Whatever the indignity may be, there are times to confront and times to sacrifice. Times to lay down our lives and preferences, choosing to be last rather than first (Matthew 20:16), and times to seek justice.

But even if we choose or feel led to respond to these moments with grace, humility, and personal sacrifice, it doesn't mean it is selfish to want to be treated with respect. Sometimes taking even a gentle stand is really worthwhile. Often it comes with a cost, relationally or financially. Personally, I now go most places prepared to pay for my own room.

Something to remember in this delicate dance is how often the perceived injustice is actually an expression of envy. We can be so deficient in our vocabulary for praising singleness that we overlook how our singleness appears advantageous to others. We may even neglect to see, and have grace for, the jealousy that lurks behind criticism of the liberties we enjoy. The more realistically I consider my singleness, the more I can also see the downsides, or at least the realities, of non-singleness. Sometimes those who express sentiments against my freedom may actually be experiencing the shadow side of coupledom.

As someone who's spent her adulthood on the outside of couples looking in, and much of her singleness pining for a partner, it has been hard for me to imagine that those people might actually want what I have.

One of my married friends once expressed jealousy of how much freedom I had to socialize without worrying about leaving a spouse behind. "She's jealous of *me*?" I puzzled. Upon reflection, though, I see more clearly how challenging it can be for married couples to balance their social energies. Similarly, as one who grew up in a postmodern culture where marriage isn't the only choice for a woman, it took a long time before I read remorse in my grandma's habitual questioning about my relationship status in light of my job, realizing that maybe she would have liked to have had the chance to work for a living. And at work, when I take off my envy goggles, I realize that I'm often the one in the break room with the most interesting stories of things I did over the weekend.

My eyes continue to open to the difficulties that can lie on the other side of the aisle. I frequently watch as strong women and men sacrifice their independence and ambition in service to their families. I'm all at once inspired, jealous, and relieved. I see couples more in love than I can ever imagine being, but they're also more restricted, patient, yielding, and submissive than I normally have to be. I notice as friends struggle to negotiate chores, travel, and budget plans with a partner and realize how delightfully inexperienced I am at the kind of compromise that must require. Sometimes I even giggle softly when my married friends get into little spats over mundane subjects and whisper to myself, "Thank God I'm single."

Recognized or not, being single is pretty awesome. As with so many things, the blessings can be scaled from the small to the monumental, the seemingly shallow to the remarkably deep. I always get the side of the bed I want, the seat on the sofa I prefer, and I have full control over the remote, the thermostat, and the music selection. My possessions and furniture are always to be found just where I left them and in the condition I left them in. I don't have to explain my credit card purchases to anyone or share in another's debt, and I can plan my financial future around only one set of goals—mine!

I can stay late at work without considering the relational or scheduling implications. I can passionately pursue my bucket list and plan my dream vacations with minimal compromise. I don't ask permission before making social engagements and have full autonomy over my response to plans involving people or activities that I don't like. I don't negotiate over the décor or paint colours in any of the rooms of my apartment, nor do I fear having prized sentimental possessions donated to the thrift store behind my back.

And oh my goodness, the closet space! It's all mine!

I cheer for the sports teams I want to without risking relational peril. I never have to agree with anyone on politics. I see the movies I want to see with little negotiation and without fear of someone cashing in on some romcom versus action movie IOU. I can comment on the attractiveness of the restaurant server, pharmacist, or lead actor in a movie without worrying about making someone jealous. And while I have to manage my own sex drive, I don't have to respond to someone else's. I can ignore my own appearance at home without being concerned that the magic is gone.

I only have to negotiate with one set of family during the holidays and I've never had to deal with having to impress or handle difficult in-laws. I can put on a little holiday weight or drink the wine that makes me breakout without worrying about how my nakedness will be perceived by anyone other than a mirror or a doctor. I can eat the garlic, onions, beans, and dairy products without concern for how the digestive results may impact another nose.

I only have to clean up after one person, and sometimes I don't clean up at all. I can shop for and cook only food I like to eat. I don't fight over leftovers, chores, storage space, toothpaste tube squeezing procedures, or toilet seat or paper roll placement. I don't have to schedule my showers, compete for bathroom time, or seek out privacy for personal moments. I can go an entire day without speaking to anyone, simply by staying home and ignoring the phone, or I can fill my life with social engagements considering only my own level of energy. I can take five minutes or five hours to get ready to go out without explaining it to anyone.

I've never justified my shoe collection or my entertainment budget to anyone but God. My sleep is rarely interrupted—I don't even know if I snore—and I can toss and turn and hog the blankets all I want while being in control of the room lighting, temperature, and linens. I can pack my schedule with work, hobbies, social activities, and volunteering, or I can binge-watch three seasons of a show over the course of a weekend. I can skip ahead in amusement parks to the single rider line.

I can respond in the moment to an internal prompting or whim without having to convince someone else of its merits. Even when I consider the time I spend serving others, most of my life is spent doing things I want or have chosen to do. If I did all these things in the context of a coupled relationship, they may be selfish. But as a single, these are simply the upsides of flying solo.

This isn't always easy to identify or explain. Sometimes singles have a different vocabulary or way of being in the world. Some can't afford to live alone while others choose not to out of family connection or a deeper need for regular human exposure. But adults who have roommates or live with family are often stigmatized as being emotionally or financially immature.

Similarly, singles are often accused of avoiding commitment. While that might be true for some, the reality is that our relationship to commitment may just be valued differently. In fact, the same characteristics and traits that forge long-term romance also forge long-term singleness. While we value and praise long-term committed relationships as significant accomplishments, we seldom acknowledge the work, faith, and self-denial it takes to be a single person who relies on God's will and timing, turns down unhealthy dating opportunities, and overcomes personal desires and urges. Just because these things don't result in romance doesn't mean they don't require commitment.

The truth is that we're capable of sacrifice, dedication, and focus, but a single doesn't always need to have the same kind of five-year plan as someone who balances their spouse's career and kids' school opportunities. Some of the joy of singleness may actually be in the commitment to flexibility, knowing that one can make significant and sudden changes without a lot of notice, negotiation, or impact on others. Whereas a commitment is a benefit to someone with roots, it can be an unnecessary hindrance to someone with wings.

When you have existing commitments, such as family, considering other options is like comparing the greener grass of another yard to the property you've already purchased. But when you haven't settled down in that way, considering other options is simply the joy and freedom of shopping the real estate market. Also, remember that sometimes our seeming lack of commitment—switching churches, for example—may actually be a result of us looking for friends.

Another thing I don't think is accounted for enough when considering the values or behaviours of singles who are also celibate is how much of our discipline quota is used up in applying ourselves to sexual purity. Research has shown that willpower is like a muscle, and there are limits to how much we can exercise in a given timeframe. While Christ can empower us to do things beyond our capacity, I think it's hubris for one who has access to frequent sexual release to judge those pursuing abstinence for other ways in which they may lapse in matters of self-discipline. In other words, *you* try being abstinent for multiple years before judging a single person for their shoe fetish or video game habits.

It may require a shift in focus to find the blessings in your single state. As with so many fruits of discipline, practice makes better. The good news is that our brains have a way of looking for what we tell them to, the same way they start to notice all the Honda Civics on the road as soon as we start shopping for one. You can use that same condition for good or evil by choosing what you keep track of and give power to. What we focus on grows.

You may need to focus on and keep track of the positive aspects of being single for a while before you see it as a gift. For me, it took a lot of deliberate reframes of gratitude before I got the hang of it. The empty bed I once complained about is now the legroom in which I delight. Bemoaning having to cook for one happens in a kitchen that is nearly always clean. The anxiety I feel about being responsible for all my own expenses has become the passion that fuels my charitable donations, investment strategies, travel plans, and shopping sprees. The fact that I have no one immediately available to care for me when I'm sick also means that I don't have to worry about being contagious or attempt to be a courteous sneezer. What's more, it means that I've never had to summon the fortitude to face the herculean task of nursing someone else's man-cold.

I realize that some of these blessings are subjective and don't apply to all singles, such as those who don't live alone or who have work, income, and family obligations which vary from mine, but my point is simple: there are rewards to be found in singleness, especially for those who seek them.

I also recognize that gender, class, ethnicity, and other elements of socioeconomic status play into this. For some, singleness isn't a choice between codependence and independence, but a choice between provision and poverty. Maybe your free time is spent working multiple jobs just to make ends meet. Having the option to consider a lack of coupledom as a romantic deficit rather than a financial one is an advantage.

For those who are both single and independent, my question may be even more powerful. Why waste the privilege of singleness on wishing for coupledom? Why waste the privilege at all?

I'm still learning how to balance service and sacrifice with advocacy and dignity when it comes to standing in my singleness. I can now set clearer boundaries around the luxuries I enjoy and am no longer as passive in responding to criticism surrounding my freedom, nor apologetic about benefiting from it. I've also learned to genuinely celebrate others' engagement and birth announcements rather than harbouring bitterness for the life I don't have. I've discovered compassion and empathy for the sincere amount of work and self-sacrifice it must take to do life as a spouse.

While I'm sure some people live their singleness in selfish or juvenile ways, the terms aren't inherently synonymous. The tendency of singleness may be towards selfishness, the same way the tendency of marriage may be towards stagnancy, but neither are necessarily true and both require surrender. When we stop conflating marriage with maturity, we are left to enjoy what is amazing about being unattached without considering it to be irresponsible.

It's possible to contribute to society, hold jobs, serve our communities, engage socially, deepen spiritually, respond empathically, manage financial and legal affairs, and generously give of our resources and talents all while getting to relish in the parts of adulthood that we always dreamed of when we were children: ice cream for dinner, not cleaning our rooms, and staying up well past our bedtimes.

CHAMPAGNE MOMENTS

*He is a wise man who does not grieve for the
things which he has not, but rejoices
for those which he has.*[44]
— Epictetus

I WAS ONCE gifted a bottle of Dom Perignon as a housewarming present with instructions to save the bottle for a significant moment: an engagement or something equally substantial. I hung on to that bottle for a long time, comparing any significant moment in my life to the anticipated momentous occasion that would be getting engaged.

I know the gift was never meant to accompany the guilt I attached to it, but over the many years of not being engaged that followed I gingerly packed that bottle and brought it to each new apartment, wondering with every new job and accomplishment whether what I was experiencing was truly champagne-worthy.

The advantage of toting around a bottle of bubbly for nearly a decade was that I always took note of reasons to celebrate. But the lesson I learned is that I can miss out on many glorious moments if I limit my view of what's worthy of acknowledgment.

There are many built-in excuses to celebrate non-singles. Couples get engagement parties, bachelor/ette parties, wedding showers and weddings, and subsequent anniversaries. Parents get birth announcement and gender reveal parties, baby showers, Mother's Day and Father's Day gatherings, kids' birthdays, plus school pageants, sporting events, and graduation ceremonies. These come alongside Valentine's Day, New Year's Eve, and even non-relationship-based holidays that can emphasize romance both on the day and in the lead-up in terms of photoshoots, gift registries, music, marketing, and décor.

But greeting cards don't congratulate you on assembling your first piece of furniture alone. People don't buy you presents for acing a test or finally hitting a new fitness milestone. Nobody takes you for dinner the first time you sign legal papers by yourself or travel independently. Friends may not spring for a babysitter so they can join you to toast your promotion at work. Celebrating singles takes intentionality and vigilance.

In the movie *The Holiday*, Kate Winslet's character, Iris, is trying to recover from a toxic romantic entanglement by doing a house-swap vacation. She soon befriends an elderly neighbour and former film producer named Arthur. After hearing her pour out her unrequited love story, Arthur gently scolds her for acting like a supporting character in her own life.

"You're supposed to be the leading lady of your own life, for God's sake!" she replies in a moment of epiphany.[45]

Too many of us singles are out there waiting for our big break, for our "real" lives to start, rather than embracing the roles we are in now. We too could be accused of playing a supporting role in arenas where we should be stepping up and stepping in to greater purpose. This may show up in the form of a boring life now, or an overdeveloped fantasy about what life could look like later. Some may even leave locations unvisited and activities unexperienced in the hopes of preserving them for a future romance.

I was one of those people who didn't want to go to a certain restaurant or destination or try a particular activity because I was saving those things for a future partner. I have let fancy dishes sit in storage for the day when I would use them as a homemaker.

But storing up celebrations for a future that may never arrive, or worrying that life may run out of delights altogether, is actually a symptom of having a scarcity mindset. In light of our abundant, rejuvenating God, this seems silly and maybe even sinful.

I no longer pin all my hopes on the concept of finding true love. I have learned instead to embrace the part of me that will always be a hopeless romantic by enjoying the enchanted moments of the present.

So here is my advice for everyone in the singleverse: don't put your life on hold!

One of the consequences of planning a life around a non-existent spouse is that we can let ourselves become boring. But as Donald Miller shares in a book he subtitled "what I learned while editing my life" it's never too late to live a better story.[46] Each of us can celebrate the beauty of life, intentionally make moments more powerful and memorable, and learn to become more interesting.

These skills were much easier as a child. Younger me let her imagination roam free. She could be a mermaid, a princess, a warrior, a scientist, a teacher, or a world-class musician. She could build fortresses out of tree branches and pinecones, or castles out of bedsheets and sofa cushions. She was rarely bored, even when alone, because she was endlessly amused by her own jokes, entertained by her own stories, and moved by her own music.

But the pressures of adulthood can grind the innocence out of us. They make us too embarrassed to be silly, too practical for daydreams, too reasonable to chase adventure. The burden of singleness can cause us to forfeit some of the romance of just living, and it might take some practice to revive our appetites for a good story.

I remember the morning I woke up early with my roommate to watch the royal wedding of the Duke and Duchess of Cambridge. From a time zone eight hours behind, we "attended" in our pyjamas with a proper English feast of Earl Grey tea, biscuits, and crumpets with creme fresh and blackberry compote. I can't profess to be a diehard royalist, and I'm aware the exact same footage was available to watch online and on about a dozen other networks during regular viewing hours, but for whatever reason it struck me as something I wanted to have more than a vague recollection of.

I don't remember much about the workday that followed that particular all-nighter. To be honest, I don't remember many details about the wedding either, but anytime someone mentions William and Kate, I fondly recall that crazy time when I got up in the middle of the night, ate scones with my roommate, showered during commercial breaks, and went to work exhausted, just to be one of the millions watching the wedding of the century live. It was a story for the sake of having a story—and I'm glad I did it!

Since awakening to the dysfunction caused by waiting for marriage to start my life, I have become a story and celebration seeker. One year, which I dubbed the Karissa Adventures, I subscribed to any email list I could think of that sold tickets, funnelling any discretionary income I could afford towards attending concerts, plays, comedy performances, sporting events, or any other activity I wanted to try.

These are habits I try to continue. I also take art and cooking classes in addition to trying all sorts of group fitness and dance-adjacent lessons, singing in choirs, and performing in bands and improv troupes.

I regularly partake in local tourist attractions. I make sure my birthday is an event. I'm not above karaoke or crafting. I cheer wildly for the blue team at local sporting events. I dress up in my fanciest clothes to go to the ballet or symphony. And I'm blessed to have cultivated a circle of friends who are willing to do some of these things with me. I've even been seen in a horse-drawn carriage in a ball gown for a friend's birthday.

My singleness is a gift I give myself when I use it to live a better story, and it becomes a gift I give to others when I take on the role of celebrationist—any excuse for a party, any effort for an anecdote. This requires both intentionality in loving my friends and giving myself permission to love myself. I've made it my mission to be the person in my circle of influence to whom people most want to tell their good news. Some of this is just about drinking in small moments. The rest is about intentionally making memories, or at least being part of someone else's.

I've stopped waiting for people to throw me parties and have started to become someone who celebrates her own success and the success of others. Whether for me or someone else, I try not to let a promotion, new job, big move, academic achievement, athletic accomplishment, therapeutic breakthrough, key birthday, or friendiversary go by without buying a drink, meal, present, card, or flowers. I want the people I love to know that their accomplishments are valued, their milestones are worthy of regard, and their lives merit a pause in recognition. I want me to know that my life will be a celebration even if no one else is around to join the party.

I have also begun to value myself and my time more. I realized that I don't have to be run ragged with children and family in order to ask or pay for cleaning and cooking services. Far too many of us have learned to tie our worth to our status, whether relationship, parental, or otherwise. We feel we have to earn our rest, justify self-care, and find our suffering further along an imaginary spectrum when compared with others.

But under the grace of a risen Saviour, none of us is tasked with having to earn our dignity or prove our worth. The busy parent who's looking for a few moments to call their own, the overworked businessperson who wishes for a clean apartment, or the avid enthusiast who wants more time for adventure are all worthy of love, attention, care, and maybe maid service.

Celebration is very much an art. Some people are so good at it that they're the first you seek to share good news with, while others have to invest great amounts of energy into simply not raining on another's parade. If you've not been in the habit of celebrating others or yourself, it may feel foreign at first and require some practice. Don't let a lack of comfort or familiarity with rejoicing become the excuse for inaction. Your first attempts at compliments, invitations, and joy may feel contrived and inauthentic, but consistent application will rewire your brain and instruct your heart towards permanent change.

It was momentous for so many reasons when, upon the completion of my master's degree, I hosted my own graduation party. I invited as many family and friends who were willing to join me for a steak dinner at a fancy restaurant after the afternoon of photos in my cap and gown. It wasn't only the pinnacle of my academic achievement and associated years of sacrifice, but a statement that I was worth celebrating.

The night before the ceremony, my immediate family crowded into the kitchenette of my hotel room with dollar-store plastic goblets. It was there that I surrendered my dusty bottle of Dom in the service of a true champagne moment—toasting the success of a woman who had become a celebrated friend.

SEEN

*To see and to be seen. That is the truest
nature of love.[47]*
—Brené Brown

NOT TOO LONG ago, when someone would ask me how I felt about being single, I would sigh and grouchily reply, "I think I'm kind of over being single... I'm just totally singled out!" God has redeemed those words for me. He has shown me that he has actually singled me out, set me apart to live a better story than any I could have hoped to have asked him for.

This continues to be a journey. A journey through grieving the life I wanted to embracing the life I actually have. A journey from rejecting and resisting the experiences that didn't fit my plan to radically accepting both myself and the path God has laid out for me. This freedom from ideas and frameworks that limited my life has opened me up to God's eternal possibilities. My path has led me beyond the mere survival of the stigma of singleness to true thriving.

The world offers two extremes for the one seeking fulfillment: either romantic love or total self-sufficiency. This binary leads people into bondage.

The Christian single must choose a third way of freedom between the extremes and manage the tensions between codependence and independence, between *"It is not good for the man to be alone"* (Genesis 2:18) and *"It is good for them to stay unmarried"* (1 Corinthians 7:8), between being obsessed with getting married and being a bitter spinster or curmudgeonly bachelor, between a restrictive sexual ethic that only views you as a prospective spouse and an extreme sexualization of culture that treats you as a sum of your urges, between satisfying desires for romance, partnership, and parenthood in the context of a spiritual family and holding space for the act of desiring out of faith in the eternity to come.

It takes courage to live this journey. Courage to be curious, wrestle, and manage the tension. Courage to be vulnerable, to hope and see what's possible. Courage to find joy, let dreams shift and grow, and let some of these dreams go altogether to make room for new ones. It takes courage to choose the happiness of presence in the face of an unknown future.

I still notice the old couple holding hands as they stroll the boardwalk, and I hope I will be that adorably romantic and in love in my sunset years. But now I also see the groups of friends—hair greyed by the wisdom of years, skin weathered and wrinkled by both pain and laughter—gathered around beach fires, lining up at the movies, and giggling across bistro tables, and I imagine me and my friends continuing our companionship and stories with vigour and determination and fun. I envision both the family I might get to raise and the many people whose lives I may be able to minister to in the liberty of a lifetime of unfettered mission. In the freedom of God's sovereignty, I can imagine multiple possible futures and know that any of them will be worthy, and difficult, and good.

I still sometimes hope for marriage, but my hope is no longer *in* marriage. I now see it as the microcosm it is, the hint of a grander narrative and greater love. It's not so much that I've given up the concept of a happy ending; rather, I've come to want more out of life than an ending.

If the point of intimate partnership is to have someone to love and bear witness to your life, then the ultimate question isn't "will you ever get married?" but rather, "are you willing to be seen?"

Humanity has a long history of hiding. In the Garden of Eden, Adam and Eve were truly seen by God. They saw him, walked with him, and had no barriers, physical or otherwise, in their access to him. In thinking they knew better, they failed to trust God's sovereignty and forfeited this intimacy through an act of disobedience.

> Then the man and his wife heard the sound of the Lord God as he was walking in the garden in the cool of the day, and they hid from the Lord God among the trees of the garden. But the Lord God called to the man, "Where are you?"
>
> He answered, "I heard you in the garden, and I was afraid because I was naked; so I hid."
>
> And he said, "Who told you that you were naked?" (Genesis 3:8–11)

The first consequence of sin was losing the ability to appear fully before God without shame—in other words, to be fully seen. It wasn't until God came back in human form, in his own vulnerability and nakedness, that this intimacy could be restored.

God desires intimacy with you. He sent his son to tear down the walls and the curtain that prevented a mutual knowing (Matthew 27:51). He longs to connect with you directly. He doesn't want anything to act as an obstruction, any relationship to act as cover, any earthly obligation to be an excuse that could prevent you from knowing him fully or being fully known.

When I stopped looking for God to meet my needs through marriage, I started realizing how often he meets me directly, how frequently he prompts me, uses me, encourages me, and seemingly lines up the universe in ways I cannot dismiss as mere coincidence. The more I lean into this familiarity, the more it grows. I treasure this intimacy, the ongoing dialogue of an unceasing prayer, the enduring peace of his Spirit so near. He never leaves me. He is the subject of my worship and respondent of my prayers.

But more often than not, he shows up in my everydayness in a quiet but constant conversation. The deeper this relationship grows, the more I resist the idea of being distracted from it, the more comfortable I am with not covering myself up, and the more reluctant I am to forfeit it for anything else.

God is a pursuer. We neither have to prove our worthiness to him or sulk in the shadows hoping he will take notice. We don't need to beautify the parts of ourselves that seem less dateable, marketable, or desirable to be in his presence. We don't have to amplify our charisma, dial back our baggage, tone down our personality, or feign reduced intelligence so that he will feel more secure. He will never tire of spending time with us. There is no quality, trait, or quirk that will cause him to "swipe left" and overlook us. We can never be too much. He wants us to come to him just as we are. He already loves us that way, already died for us that way, already did everything that would be needed to have perfect unity with us. As a friend of mine says it, "We may never run out of ways to need his mercy, but he will never run out of new mercies to give."

God doesn't buy in to our marriage prep mask or dating persona. He knows that it's all a front. He was there when we made the mess we are now trying to cover up, and he already committed to the long haul of covenant when he went to the cross. He committed to the highs and the lows, the good and bad, the beautiful and the ugly, the times of confidence and those when things are falling apart.

He is love, and a love that doesn't scare easily. This love is both divine and superhuman. It's capable of drowning out the noise of rejection, tempering the insecurity of perfectionism, and injecting courage into the faintest of hearts. It's strong enough to burn away that which would rob us of joy and resurrect the most deadened of hopes. It models the way of surrender and yet calls us to always endure. In this love, we need not fear the risk of community or the quiet of solitude.

> Love is patient, love is kind. It does not envy,
> it does not boast, it is not proud. It does not
> dishonor others, it is not self-seeking, it is not
> easily angered, it keeps no record of wrongs. Love
> does not delight in evil but rejoices with the truth.
> It always protects, always trusts, always hopes,
> always perseveres. (1 Corinthians 13:4–7).

God sees you. He loves you. He knows you better than you know yourself. His spirit is within you (Romans 8:9). He is speaking and singing over you (Zephaniah 3:17). He wants you to know that he hears your cry, knows your heart, and has both a present for you to relish and a future in store.

Can you let him love you? Can you invite him into your brokenness, confusion, vulnerability, loneliness, flaws, and fear? Can you drop the act, the robe, the loincloths you think are helping you be more secure? Can you share with him your dreams, joys, hopes, and flourishing? Do you see him? Will you let him see you? Will you allow him to single you out?

A LETTER TO TWENTY-YEAR-OLD ME

DEAR TWENTY-YEAR-OLD ME,

The big question I know you have for me is, "Am I married?" The answer is no. I know that lands with a wallop, so go ahead: catch your breath, cry a little, and then hang in with me.

You probably won't believe me when I say that it's so much better than you think, but maybe you can consider what might be possible for you now that you know that singleness is a guarantee for your foreseeable future. Now that you are one hundred percent sure that you will live to forty without being married, how can that help you make decisions? What can you start or stop doing? What good changes can you make?

I have some suggestions.

Don't put your life on hold! Adulthood doesn't begin at marriage, so start yours now. You are clinging to one definition of happiness. Though you come by this honestly, it will make you miserable if you let it. There is so much more to life than finding a spouse, and your life will be more purposeful, fulfilling, and peaceful the faster you figure that out. Don't waste your next decade asking God for a life you think you want rather than enjoying the life he has already given you. I know that you believe he has plans for you, but believe that they are good plans too. He will make use of all your hopes, desires, skills, and experiences in ways you don't think are possible right now.

The reason I can say all of this so confidently is that I also know the answer to the second question I'm guessing that you have for me: "Am I happy?" Yes. You are strong, talented, loved, and can—and will—do a lot with your single life. I know you fear not saving room for a spouse or becoming too independent or selfish to be loved. But I would challenge you to stop thinking of your life in terms of how it's shaping you for a future marriage. Consider how it might be shaping you as a child of God. Start living a life of purpose now. Love always makes room. So love your God, love your family, love your friends, love those who need love, and love yourself.

Knowing that you will have this freedom, this gift, this responsibility, and yes, this sometimes-burden of singleness, what might you try? Where might you live? What might you learn? What are you aching in your core to do that you thought you would only do "after?" Don't wait! Don't fear the dreams. Don't hate the hope. Dive in.

There is work to do, there are people to be loved, there are friends to be made, there are hurts to be healed, there are problems to be solved, and there is a heavenly kingdom bursting forth on the earth. There are far more successes, adventures, and experiences to be embraced than you have thought possible.

It's true that your life doesn't look anything like you thought it would. It's better!

TRULY LOVED

THE WEEK IS mostly about retreating, a breathe-in-breathe-out, nowhere-to-be, delightfully slow-paced kind of indulgence. Somewhere around hour ninety-six of the reflecting, journaling, worshipping, conversing, and nature-gazing, all of which have me wondering how I can be so lucky to be on a writing retreat, I realize that it might be the longest consecutive amount of time I've ever felt so contented, a realization over which I breathe a deep sigh of gratitude. This reflection, along with a few sunny dips in the infinity pool, allow memories to bubble to the surface of my mind: my first diary entry, my heart many times broken and revived, what I wanted to be when I grew up, the delight of hearing God's voice.

After I enjoy the sun, water, food, and conversation, I set aside my leisure and I write. I instruct both the achingly tearful and joyously warm recollections to pour out of my heart, through my fingers, and across my keyboard to the pages of my burgeoning book. I earnestly attempt to communicate all I have learned about the pain, joy, and humour of being alive.

And when I run out of stories and teachings, and sparkling water, I look up and take in my surroundings: ocean, mountains, forest, wildlife. I close my eyes to better hear the music they make as God's creation weaves a melody that reminds me of a simple truth: life is beautiful.

Because regardless of where I've come from, where I'm going, or what tomorrow holds, I know it will be good. As here, beneath the weight of my laptop, next to my mug of Earl Grey tea, I sit.

Single.

Loved.

ACKNOWLEDGEMENTS

IN SEVERAL WAYS, the content of this book was crowdsourced. As an extravert, writing requires conversation before I commit ideas to paper, and I am immensely grateful to the many who have helped me piece together the fragments of these pages over the years. If you were single and in my life at some point before publishing this, your fingerprints are on these pages somewhere, but thanks to those who explicitly shared their stories and wisdom that I hope will now benefit so many others. I extend special appreciation to the older single men and women in my life who have graciously modelled the way regardless of how ungraciously I may have followed.

I'm especially thankful to my family (Phil, Linda, Amberia, Kaitlyn, Damian, and Courtney) and friends (Christina, Kim, and the many other incredible women and men I know who are too numerous to name individually) for showing me the fullest potential of human love, for the hours of discussion and prayer, and for being the reasons I knew singleness could be amazing. This includes Elisa, Ashley, Lindsay, and Marie, who were also early content reviewers.

Thanks also to my social media community for sharing their stories and to my church for helping me get brave enough to share mine.

I specifically thank Mark Buchanan for planting the seeds of writing a book all those years ago and for watering those seeds with mentorship, coaching, and retreats. Thank you, Karen Stiller, for your belief, promotion, and platforming of my writing and encouragement to continue the publishing journey. To Emily Walker, thank you for your guidance and support on all things related to brand. Thanks also to Word Alive Press and the Braun Book Award committee for allowing these words to finally become a published work.

And lastly, shoutouts to all the men who friend-zoned me: this book would literally not exist without you.

ENDNOTES

1 Paulo Coelhol, *X*. April 18, 2012 (https://x.com/paulocoelho/status/192573337921269760).

2 Phillips Brooks, as cited in: John C. Maxwell, *Talent Is Never Enough: Discover the Choices That Will Take You beyond Your Talent* (Nashville, TN: Nelson Business, 2007), 19.

3 Albert Einstein, Infeld Léopold, and Walter Isaacson, *The Evolution of Physics: From Early Concepts to Relativity and Quanta* (New York, NY: Simon & Schuster, 2007), 92.

4 Aaron Sorkin, *The West Wing*. Season 3, episode 3, "Ways and Means." Directed by Alex Graves. Aired October 24, 2001.

5 As Timothy Keller and Katherine Leary Alsdorf write, idolatry "means turning a good thing into an ultimate thing" (*Every Good Endeavor: Connecting Your Work to Gods Work* [New York, NY: Penguin Books, 2016], 132).

6 Anne Ju, "Courage Is the Most Important Virtue, Says Writer and Civil Rights Activist Maya Angelou at Convocation," *Cornell Chronicle*. May 24, 2008 (http://news.cornell.edu/stories/2008/05/courage-most-important-virtue-maya-angelou-tells-seniors).

7 "St. Irenaeus of Lyons," *Taizé*. Date of access: May 26, 2019 (https://www.taize.fren_article6431.html).

8 Aristotle, *Nicomachean Ethics*, 2nd ed., trans. Terence Irwin (Indianapolis, IN: Hackett Publishing, 1999), 140.

9 James Strong, *Strong's Expanded Exhaustive Concordance of the Bible* (Nashville, TN: Thomas Nelson, 2009), #5486.

10 Erwin McManus, "Clear Eyes, Full Hearts, Can't Lose," *YouTube*. April 22, 2018 (https://www.youtube.com/watch?v=SNoCKG7k7qc).

11 Andy Stanley, "Trading Your Future for Lusts." October 31, 2017 (https://preachitteachit.org/sermons/trading-your-future-for-lusts).

12 Strong, *Strong's Expanded Exhaustive Concordance of the Bible*, #4561.

13 Thomas Lewis, Fari Amini, and Richard Lannon, *A General Theory of Love* (New York, NY: Vintage Books, 2001.

14 C. S. Lewis, *Mere Christianity* (New York, NY: HarperOne, 2001), 120.

15 I heard Dr. Darrell Johnson preach this message, "On Earth as It Is in Heaven," live in Vancouver on March 30, 2019.

16 J.K. Rowling, *Harry Potter and the Philosopher's Stone* (London, UK: Bloomsbury, 2014), 230.

17 George Herbert, "The Pulley," *Poetry Foundation*. Date of access: January 6, 2025 (https://www.poetryfoundation.org/poems/44370/the-pulley).

18 David Foster Wallace, "This Is Water," *Farnam Street*. Date of access: January 6, 2025 (https://fs.blog/david-foster-wallace-this-is-water).

19 Bruce Marshall, "The World, The Flesh, and Father Smith," *Nanotube*. Date of access: January 6, 2025 (https://nanotube.msu.edu/WFFS).

20 Stephen Chbosky, *The Perks of Being a Wallflower* (New York, NY: MTV Books/Gallery Books, 2012), 24.

21 Joshua Harris, *I Kissed Dating Goodbye* (Sisters, OR: Multnomah, 2003).

22 Jane Austen, *Pride and Prejudice* (London, UK: T. Egerton, 1813).

23 Dr. Seuss, *Dr. Oh, the Places You Will Go* (New York, NY: Random House, 1990), 2.

24 "Welcome," Steven C. Hayes, PhD. April 30, 2019 (stevenchayes.com/about).

25 C.S. Lewis, *The Chronicles of Narnia* (New York, NY: Harper Collins, 2001), 146.

26 Williamson, Marianne. *A Return to Love: Reflections on the Principles of a Course in Miracles* (New York, NY: HarperOne, 1992), 190-191.

27 Elaine Hoan and Geoff MacDonald, "'Sisters Are Doin' It for Themselves': Gender Differences in Singles' Well-Being," *Social Psychological and Personality Science 0(0)*. October 24, 2024.

28 Mark Buchanan, "Community Engagement." Victoria Church of the Nazarene, Victoria BC, Feb 9, 2019.

29 Carey Nieuwhof, "CNLP 222: Patrick Lencioni," *Carey Nieuwhof*. October 22, 2018 (https://careynieuwhof.com/episode222).

30 Covey, Stephen R. *The 7 Habits of Highly Effective People: Powerful Lessons in Personal Change*. New York: Simon & Schuster, 2014.

31 Andy Stanley, "Andy Stanley: Jesus Ended the Old Covenant Once and for All," *Christianity Today*. October 22, 2018 (https://www.christianitytoday.com/ct/2018/october-web-only/andy-stanley-irresistible-response-to-foster.html).

32 Monica Geyen, "Is the Church Breeding Loneliness?" *Desiring God*. May 26, 2019 (https://www.desiringgod.org/articles/is-the-church-breeding-loneliness).

33 "Alone," *Etymonline*. Date of access: January 8, 2025 (https://www.etymonline.com/word/alone)

34 John Ortberg, *Eternity Is Now in Session: A Radical Rediscovery of What Jesus Really Taught about Salvation, Eternity, and Getting to the Good Place* (Carol Stream, IL: Tyndale Momentum, 2018), 154.

35 Rupi Kaur, *Milk and Honey* (Kansas City, MO: Andrews McMeel Publishing, 2018), 161.

36 Leo Buscaglia, *Living, Loving, Learning* (New York, NY: Ballantine, 1982), 264.

37 Annie F. Downs, "That Sounds Fun, Episode 38: Andrea Lucado," *Annie F. Downs*. May 18. 2017 (https://www.anniefdowns.com/podcast/that-sounds-fun-episode-38-andrea-lucado).

38 Donne, John, *Devotions Upon Emergent Occasions* (Ann Arbor, MI: University of Michigan Press, 1953), 63.

39 Whitney Jefferson, "Amy Poehler's Awesome Harvard Speech," *Jezebel*. June 19, 2013 (https://jezebel.com/amy-poehlers-awesome-harvard-speech-5805927).

40 Brené Brown, *The Gifts of Imperfection* (Center City, MN: Hazelden, 2010), 20.

41 Rick Warren, *The Purpose Driven Life: What on Earth Am I Here For?* (Grand Rapids, MI: Zondervan, 2007), 148.

42 Kahlil Gibran, "On Friendship," *Poets.org*. Date of access: January 8, 2025 (https://poets.org/poem/friendship-1).

43 L.M. Montgomery, *Anne of Green Gables* (Boston, MA: L.C. Page & Company, 1908).

44 Epictetus, *The Discourses Of Epictetus*, trans. George Long (London, UK: George Bell and Sons, 1890), 429.

45 *The Holiday*, directed by Nancy Meyers (Los Angeles, CA: Columbia Pictures, 2006).

46 Donald Miller, *A Million Miles in a Thousand Years: What I Learned While Editing My Life* (Nashville, TN: Thomas Nelson, 2010).

47 "From Brené: On Seeing, Being Seen, and the True Nature of Love." Brené Brown. Date accessed: May 26, 2025 (https://brenebrown.com/art/to-see-and-to-be-seen-quote-card).

www.ingramcontent.com/pod-product-compliance
Lightning Source LLC
Chambersburg PA
CBHW070147100426
42743CB00013B/2839